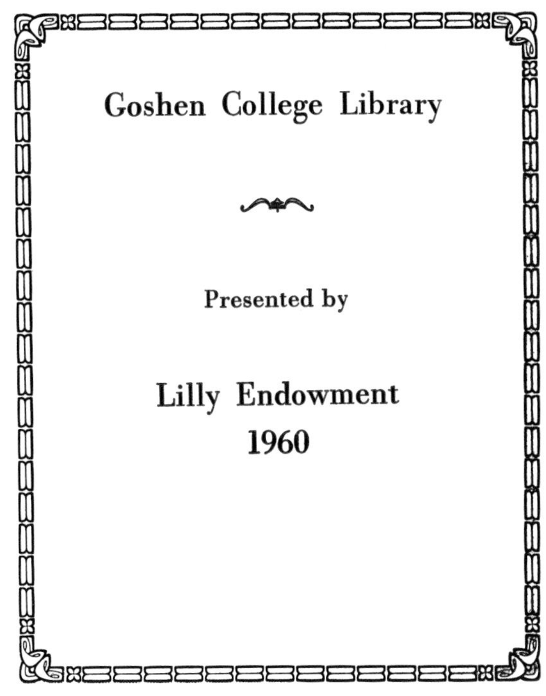

LAST MAN IN

LAST MAN IN

Racial Access to Union Power

By SCOTT GREER
NORTHWESTERN UNIVERSITY

The Free Press of Glencoe, Illinois

Printed in the United States of America

Library of Congress Catalog Card No. 59-6789

ACKNOWLEDGEMENTS

The following book and the research upon which it is based were possible only through the support of many individuals and organizations. Financially the work was supported through Sigmund Livingston Research Fellowships, with assistance from the Department of Anthropology and Sociology of the University of California at Los Angeles and from the Graduate School of Northwestern University. Intellectually, the work was supported, encouraged and criticized, by Professors Eshref Shevky, Philip Selznick, Edwin Lemert and Leonard Broom; though they may be surprised at the final result, I can detect the influence of each in these pages.

Most gratitude is due the many individuals in the Los Angeles union movement who took me into their confidence and whose anonymnity in this book is a moral imporative. They are still involved in the problems to be described and, as their indentification might affect their fortunes in solving these problems, they must be lost in the category of "informant." To me they are much more than a mere source of information to be manipulated in a formal scheme. Their careers and the moral dilemmas which they face are the living quick of the world which the organizational analyst must understand.

Unfortunately my most valuable informant need no longer remain anonymous. This book is dedicated to the memory of John J. Lyons. Jack Lyons was a labor skate, a mediator, and a man of good will. He demonstrated with intellectual and moral courage that, in the long run, there is a great advantage for the man who is willing to take the role of the other-- even with the "power boys" of massive organization.

TABLE OF CONTENTS

CHAPTER I

INTRODUCTION: ETHNIC RELATIONS AND ORGANIZATIONAL CONSTRAINT

The participation of ethnic minorities in the labor unions today is a test case. Here, in interaction, are two controversial and dynamic types of collectivity, each a storm center of modern society. Mobile in aspiration and to some degree in fact, their place in the social order ambiguous and unstable, each is in its way characteristic of large scale society. Each is a social response to a world in which the increasing scope of organization draws together in a single web of interdependence the most diverse and conflicting groups. There are few maps or charts from the past which are useful in interpreting either. They have emerged through the vast processes of rational transformation which human society is undergoing and there is little consensus on their origins, nature, or probable future.

Definitions of Labor Unions:

This lack of consensus is especially true of the labor unions. Whether seen as beneficent or malignant, they are seen and defined by all commentators as new and important centers of power in American life. In the view of one school they are the "new community," the only community existing in industrial society. Their function is to create a sense of belonging, a place for the individual (39).* Irving Howe, in his study of the United Auto Workers, has said:

> "As one looks at Detroit one must conclude that, if by some stroke of catastrophe, the UAW were removed, life in the city would be quite intolerable for those who work in its giant plants. It alone has brought a sense of human warmth into an area dominated by robots, pistons and dollars--and that, more than anything else, is the measure of its triumph."(19)

Others, however, have seen unions today as primarily anti-bodies within the industrial organization, serving to limit and define the arbitrary power in the hands of management (10). Still others view them as irresponsible agglomera-

* Numbers in parentheses refer to the terminal bibliography Appendix B

tions of power, beyond the control or consent of their members --the private preserves of powerful leaders. Certainly study after study indicates that membership in a union, even loyalty to a union, does not motivate many to attend the elections, much less the ordinary assemblies, of "their community." The general nature and function of unions remain ambiguous, though their power is tangible enough.

Such general questions make the answering of specific questions about unions more difficult, and policy toward ethnic minorities is one such question. Policy varies between International Unions, between regions for the same International, between locals in the same region and even between plants and departments within plants. Formal policy is made and remade at the conventions of the International Union and at the conventions of the federations, but operational policy in any given situation remains problematical despite such formal policy. Though the ideology of most unions is favorable to the inclusion of ethnic workers as full citizens, they are excluded completely from some of these locals and they "run the union" in others. In understanding the conditions which produce such variations the nature and functions of unions are necessarily a part of the subject for investigation.

Ethnic Minorities and the Union Movement:

The status in America of ethnic minorities, Negroes, Mexicans, Jews and foreign-born, is equally ambiguous. The growth of large-scale society creates enclaves with visible differences, cultural and otherwise, through the migration of peoples and the increasing inclusiveness of a given society. However, the resulting barriers to interaction and mobility are by no means clearly understood; the necessary and sufficient conditions for ethnic differentiation are subject to a considerable debate. To further complicate the problem, each ethnic population is changing in its characteristics while the society is changing in the position it assigns them; finally, each ethnic population is different in important respects from others. Cultural background, place and time of entry into modern society, visibility and concentration, are only some of the differences that matter.

A very large proportion of the most depressed ethnic groups such as Negroes and Mexicans is to be found in the blue-collar occupations, as manual workers; this is one aspect of their differential behavior and treatment. These are in turn occupations that are most strongly organized by the unions. In the unions, therefore, the participation of ethnic members allows one to study both the nature of unions and the behavior of ethnic populations.

Formally the unions take an uncompromising position against the differential treatment of their members on terms other than those specified in their contracts. The provision of such equal citizenship is one function of the union as such. Differential treatment of Mexicans or Negroes is then a clue to the pressures exerted upon union leaders which contradict their formal aims.

For the ethnic minorities, on the other hand, labor unions are among the most powerful mixed organizations to which they have access. Negroes and Mexicans, populations intrinsically without power in our society, have here an opportunity to organize influence. From this perspective, differential treatment or equal treatment of ethnic members should help clarify the effects of union organization upon ethnic relations.

Phrased in terms of social action the questions might stand, "What importance do ethnic minorities have, for those who wish to build a strong union movement?" Or, "How do unions affect race relations and how could they be used to help change them?" Such questions, posed in an action framework, are nevertheless useful for basic inquiry. They structure the problem area in such a way as to bring into sharp relief that which men must do, as against that which they might like to do "if things were different."

In more formal terms, the first question implies that the presence of ethnic minorities is an explanatory variable, the effect upon the labor union is then the focus of inquiry. The second question reverses the order: the structure of the union movement is the explanatory variable, and its effect upon the nature of ethnic relations is the subject to be investigated. In this inquiry both formulations will be used, but emphasis will be upon the latter. It will then be necessary to explicate, in detail, the nature of union politics.

In recent years several brilliant studies of labor unions have been carried out by Mills (26), Wilensky (40), and Lipset (23). Mills and Wilensky have emphasized the role of the union leader; they have, in effect, segregated an occupational universe and concentrated upon the population which inhabits it. Lipset and his associates have worked intensively with the internal political structure of one International Union, the International Typographical Union. Although the present study owes a great deal to these works, its approach is radically different.

Concentration upon one union organization through the case history approach used by Lipset and his associates leaves the unanswered question: How far can one generalize? What is constant and common to all unions, what is accidental and what is variable? On the other hand, a study of a broad sample of union leaders results in a relative slighting of the very organizational pressures and powers which make the union leader's role strategic for sociological inquiry. The present study is primarily concerned with just these aspects of the role. Therefore the comparative case study method has been used.

The comparative case study method requires a sample in which there is great variety in the cases used, and this variety must be manifest in those variables suspected of being determinant. With such a sample, however, it is then possible to identify the most significant structural variables and to discover empirical types which have predictive power. Such was the aim of the present inquiry. Twenty-one local labor unions were intensively analyzed; empirical types were discovered and were used to explain the variations in ethnic participation, representation and the treatment of the "race issue" by the local unions.

This study of ethnic minorities in the Los Angeles labor unions was, therefore, both an empirical charting of a relatively unknown area and an effort to clarify certain general aspects of organizational theory. The study was necessarily experimental in methodology and the subject forced the construction of new theory at the middle range, between universal generalizations applicable to all mankind, on one hand, and the report of measurements on the other.

"Attitudes" and Ethnic Relations:

The study of relations between ethnic groups, populations which, culturally varying and socially visible, have a distinctive place in the rank order of social honor, has been a preoccupation of American sociology from its inception. Yet, the study of ethnic relations has for the most part ignored any systematic study of power structure as a determinant. Instead, the focus has been upon the social psychological aspects of 'race'-- the individual images held of a given population (or "stereotypes"), the individual statement of preference (or "social distance").

Such social psychological studies have placed the emphasis upon the isolated individual in a test situation; they imply a remarkable autonomy of action for this individual. This democratic approach, (one vote to each opinionator), while admirable in some areas and, as Blumer has noted, applicable to distributive phenomena such as market behavior, is apt to be very misleading when it is applied to action in an organized field (4). It is usually related to social action and hence to the status of a given ethnic group through such concepts as "custom" or "the mores"-- broad uniformities in attitudes and images among a population. However, it is very difficult to demonstrate the connection, empirically, between the "mores" and the way organized groups behave, and the use of the "mores" as an explanatory concept blurs the important distinction between the individual as subject and the group as subject. As a result of confusion at this level, the specific action of given leadership groups is merged with such imagined entities as "public opinion" and given a legitimacy it does not deserve (12).

A statistically significant variation in the response of isolated individuals, as in the attitude test situation or the public opinion poll, may not be predictive of any significant differentiation in their overt behavior "when the chips are down." In order to translate individual reactions of this sort into predicates for _social_ action, one must know the structure within which the individual has to act. This structure is usually given; it is not created extemporaneously as an expression of individual attitudes.

Contrariwise, in using social structure as a predictive device for the behavior of a population there is no need for postulating uniformity in the mores of that population. On the contrary, much deviation may be expected in the symbolic definition of the situation and some deviation will occur in overt behavior. The minimal expectation in using the group as a predictive device is that there will usually be effective group control of overt, socially visible, behavior. This control, whether exercised through administrative decrees, common law, or informal sanctions, _may_ tend to conform to the modal definition of the situation among the group members, but it will not do so in any automatic fashion.

Organizational Structure and Ethnic Relations:

Since very little social action is a direct expression of individual attitudes, the nature of the group structure becomes a central concern in studying the status of ethnic minorities. In this frame of reference, "social distance" and "stereotypes" are frequently dependent or irrelevant factors. Concern is with the social effects of organized groups upon the ethnic minority, usually resulting from the organizational necessities of the groups involved-- unions, industry, and others.

In order to understand the status of ethnic members within a collectivity then, the internal structure of that collectivity must be known. The varieties of union control structure indicate something of the range possible and, in each variety, the degree of power and prestige possible for the ethnic contingents is different. Sheer numbers of ethnic members within an organization's membership are less important than the way the leadership-membership relations are structured. Such power-structures cannot be derived from the attitudes of the leaders, the membership, or the ethnic members of these locals.

However, as will be demonstrated at length in the description of the configurations of pressure upon union leaders, the internal organization of the local union is usually not understandable simply in terms of its constitution and formal role structure. Its foreign relations with competitors, allies, the home office or the international, frequently over-ride local demands. This is the limiting principle in using the structure of any given formally organized group as an explanatory device. The group is not self-contained and autonomous; it is dependent, for it is a differentiated segment of a total society. In these local unions such inter-collective relations were found to be of an extreme importance.

The general conclusion is unavoidable that ethnic relations and the status of ethnic minorities are usually dependent factors, rarely over-riding considerations. They may be seen as by-products of other processes not particularly "ethnic" in function. Thus, for example, the inclusion of Negroes and Mexicans in the locals of the sample is the result of hiring practices in industry and these, in turn, result from the balance between labor supply and demand. Furthermore, ethnic representation in the local's politics is also dependent upon the source of the local's power. Even to the ethnic labor leader the status of ethnic members is rarely a determinant of important decisions.

This secondary nature of ethnic issues is reinforced by inter-collective agreements; the status of ethnic groups is tied to the relative balance of power, the accomodation or conflict, between two or more organized groups. Thus in the case of captive locals, no matter how intensely the leaders may be committed to raising the status of their ethnic members, they are also committed willy-nilly to their international hierarchy and its "high level deals" with other unions. It is also a secondary consideration in democratic locals with ethnic leaders which, lacking organizational power, need the sufferance of management to survive.

These inter-collective relationships with respect to "race" tend to become structured. Accomodation results in a commitment to the other party which is not casually ignored. Once the situation is so structured it is difficult to change, for each party assumes the <u>status quo</u> and exercises pressure upon the other to perpetuate it. This occurs in relations between Southern liberals and accomodative "race leaders," between political leaders of ethnic minorities and the major political parties, and between the leaders of unions and their contracted managements. To understand the internal policy of an organization with respect to ethnic constituents, the foreign relations of that organization must be taken into account; they may determine internal relations.

The Conditional Nature of Social Power:

This leads to the following corollary: social power is always conditional. Existing only through social organization, it automatically implies the dependency of a leadership group. Such dependency is a constraint upon possible action: it reflects basic conditions for the tenure of the leaders, the existence of organizational power, or the survival of the organization. All leaders have their problems and these are usually not a choice between two goods but rather a forced choice between two necessary conditions for organizational strength. Ethnic uplift is usually a possible good, rarely a necessary condition for strength; as such, it gives precedence to the necessary.

In attempting to interpret an organization's policy towards ethnic minorities it is necessary to be very careful in attributing the status of Mexicans or Negroes to anti-Mexican and anti-Negro prejudice. Such a conspiracy theory of discrimination, while usually not explicitly held by responsible thinkers, is yet very common, because an explanation of ethnic relations as a result of "attitudes" inevitably works in reverse, placing responsibility for the depressed status of ethnic minorities upon the head (or attitude) of union leader and member. The distinction between attitude and policy is forgotten.

An organizational approach forces one to begin with the assumption that there are limits upon what any leader can do. The "practical situation" of the leader and his local will always take precedence over his ideology. Long term, humanistic values can be translated into action only when the individual understands how to do so (and this understanding is not common) and when it is not suicidal for the individual or his organization to do so. Otherwise, ideology is irrelevant.

Organization and Ideology:

While taking the burden of analysis from the subjective field of leader or members, an organizational approach allows the specification of conditions under which action will be necessary in the direction of changing the status of ethnic minorities -- whether accompanied by changes in ideology or not. The war time labor shortage is the most obvious example of such conditions. And, once a large number of ethnic individuals are in a position to exercise pressure in an organization, the ideology of that organization and its leaders will change.

The conditional nature of social power is nowhere better illustrated than in the position of the local union leaders. Such individuals are frequently portrayed in the press as autocrats; this discussion tends, perhaps, to show them in an overly helpless position. However, such leaders when acting with respect to the race issue are probably typical of most officials exposed to the dilemma. The status of ethnic minorities is a side issue, subordinate to the success and survival of the individual officer and his organization. He must play his role under threat of elimination from the position; his role is, in turn, related to other roles and, if he deviates, he automatically creates problems for his fellows. This, in its nature, reinforces the control system for, in anticipation of sanctions or in response to them, the individual-- union leader, personnel manager, or politician -- "stays in line" or gets back in line.

The role system is not, however, an idiosyncratic structure, created out of caprice or the individual attitudes of the men involved. It is, in turn, derived from the basic source of the organization's power. In more general terms, the functions which the organization performs are the basis of its hold on members, outside recognition and, hence, existence. These functions are the basis for the more or less rationalized role-system, for they are the origins of the jobs that must be done. The jobs must be done if the local stays in business; the leader must perform them to keep his job.

Social power cannot be used at will to change the status of ethnic minorities in industry, the unions, or elsewhere. It is never a free instrument-- it must be paid for. The individual union leader pays for his power by conforming to his role, reinforcing the role-system, and thus helping to secure the basic necessities of the union as an organization. He can actively promote Mexican and Negro opportunities where he does not have to renege on these primary obligations but, where there is a conflict, the ethnic issue will be second. This is most evident in the case of the Negro or Mexican union leader. Whether the local reinforces the role of the Negro as an "Uncle Tom" or is used to protect his "share" and raise his status, the individuals who control it are bound by the conditional nature of their power. This study will specify some of the conditions of local union power.

In summary; the aim of this book is to describe a particular area of social behavior, one with historical importance and value relevance, with as little distortion as possible. If this documentation is in such a form as to allow its use for testing general theories of social behavior and if those theories are useful in illuminating and defining the documentation(as well as clarifying the purpose of further investigation into these phenomena) then it should have some utility in the larger enterprise of creating an empirically grounded theory which will "make sense" out of the problems men are concerned with.

Such problems, however distorted in colloquial thought, seem to be those from which social science theory receives its initial impetus. Race riots, strikes, war and revolution, are empirical points of resistance which puncture old notions and force new hypotheses. Casual breakdowns are the starting points of most inquiry seriously concerned with the structure of human life. Such historical phenomena as those relating to the status of ethnic minorities in Los Angeles local unions and the state of democratic processes in those locals, as they point toward structure and interdependence, furnish the opportunity to move nearer an ahistorical knowledge of form and process.

CHAPTER II

UNION TYPES AND THE PATTERN OF ETHNIC JOBS

The Setting:

Los Angeles is one of the least known of the great American cities. Without literary referents (the stereotype of Hollywood obscures more than it illuminates) few individuals outside the area have any image of the metropolis, and few anywhere have a perspective from which it may be seen as a whole. Because of its rapid growth, the result of massive migration, Los Angeles as a great world city is an extremely recent phenomenon; as it is the setting for the study which follows, it must be characterized briefly (7, 21, 38).

1. Los Angeles is extremely dispersed. Even at the center of the city there are only 4,400 persons per square mile, or about one-fourth the concentration of Chicago, one-sixth that of New York. At the time of the field work for this study, four and one-half million persons were distributed over more than 2,000 square miles.

2. The population is largely made up of in-migrants. The total population in 1900 was 190,000; in 1950, four and one-half million. Most residents of any neighborhood, most members of any organization, are people from out of the State.

3. As a result, there is little hierarchy in the social structure. Because of dispersion, and the lack of a common center, the metropolitan community has no clear-cut structure of top leadership. Because of the tremendous volume of in-migration, the nature of "social class" in the Warnerian sense is as obscure to most of the inhabitants as it is to the social scientist.

4. Growth through in-migration has been of great volume for over five decades; it continues at a rapid rate. This is because of the expanding industrial structure of the area; for most of the years since 1940 the Los Angeles metropolitan area has had a "short labor supply," and a consequent demand for new workers.

Both ethnic minorities and labor unions in Los Angeles have been shaped by these factors; a major outpost of modern industrial society has attracted workers from all over the continent to the semi-desert coastal plain-- and the labor unions have followed.

Mexicans and Negros: The Principal Ethnic Groups

Mexicans and Negroes together made up over 600,000 of the Los Angeles Metropolitan Area's population in 1950. The Negro population had grown during the 1940's from 96,000 to approximately 220,000, growing at a faster rate than did the total and increasing from three and one-third per cent of all Los Angelenos to five per cent. The sharp increase was chiefly the result in in-migration, predominantly from the Southwest and the deep South.

The flood of new Negro citizens included many with lower education than the older Negro population; it brought thousands of "backwoods" Negroes into the settled Negro "black belt" community. This area, running south of the central city along Central Avenue with a salient to the west, expanded with the war migration and, after the war, the dams gave way. Rapid succession carried many Negro families into pleasant "middle class" neighborhoods. The loose organization of the city and its rapid expansion in all directions were probably important in allowing this Negro movement to take place with a minimum of friction. At any rate, though the median education and income of Los Angeles Negroes are lower than those of the total population, there was in 1950 a substantial Negro "middle class" with high school educations, working chiefly in government services and the Negro businesses-- as well as many others "doing a lifetime at hard labor."

While a very large part of the present Negro population is made up of recent migrants, the Mexican population is chiefly made up of older migrants and native children of the earlier migrations. It is estimated that Mexicans amounted to over 200,000 (or one-tenth of the population) before Pearl Harbor; in 1950 the total was over 400,000. Thus the Mexican population kept its relative status as a part of the whole; however, a great deal of the increase was the result of high fertility in a traditional, family-oriented culture. Thus it should not be assumed that Mexicans in Los Angeles are chiefly foreign-born. Although they are a large proportion of all foreign-born in the city, nearly eighty per cent of all California Mexicans are native-born Americans and one-third are "native sons of native sons."

Mexicans are less highly concentrated residentially than are Negroes in Los Angeles (though they are still five times as concentrated as would be expected if there were no segregation) and they live scattered in dozens of enclaves throughout the County (37). They are found in the outlying towns such as San Fernando, Torrance and El Monte, as well as in the highly congested urban neighborhoods of the near East Side. Their occupational and educational level is in general somewhat lower than that of Negroes and considerably below that of white non-ethnics. There is a gradual movement upward in occupational level and education going from the foreign-born to their children and their children's children, but it is a slow movement. In 1950 the median income for Mexican households was approximately one-half that for the total population while the size of the average Mexican family was considerably larger.

Although there was a small population of "Spaniards" predating the settlement of Americans in Southern California, Mexicans first entered in large numbers with the labor shortage of World War I. They came from the villages and small towns of the less urbanized Mexican states as well as westward from Texas, Arizona and New Mexico. With little occupational background in modern industry they entered the job market at the lowest levels. They worked as laborers on the railway "section gangs," in large scale farming, in such dirty industries as meat packing, foundry work and brick and clay manufacturing (17). They brought with them, not the Negro's heritage of long experience as a depressed racial minority, but a folk culture and social expectations based upon very low socio-economic rank. Their alien culture and language and their low economic status combined to make them extremely vulnerable to the disorders that attend group poverty in a modern city.

Although there are sharp differences between these two ethnic groups they share many aspects of a common situation. They are the "insulted and injured" who have left the land of their birth and heritage in response to the expanding economic system, the increasing wealth, of Los Angeles. Finally, they have moved into a labor movement, an organizational structure peculiar to modern urban man, a reflection of his grappling with the long-term changes from status to contract--changes which they have experienced so vividly through incorporating history into their personal life spans.

The Los Angeles Labor Movement:

They moved, not into an abstract organizational system, but into a specific labor movement, a given congeries of groups at a given time. The Los Angeles labor movement also has its history.

Although it is an old movement it has had an extremely erratic history of growth and decline. A powerful force in the first decade of the century, it faced powerful enemies in the business elites of the County. Although it appeared, for a brief time, that the movement might succeed in organizing the city as San Francisco was organized, the bombing of the *Times* building and the power of the united anti-labor forces was too much for the amorphous alliance of craft unions. In 1910, even with substantial aid from the San Francisco unions, the Los Angeles movement was crushed. For thirty years the "City of the Angels" was also the "citadel of the open shop"; the Los

Angeles movement was a movement in name only-- an alliance of a few strong craft unions in areas of extreme technological monopoly.

The contemporary union movement in Los Angeles, then, has some roots in the past, but for most purposes its birth can be dated in the last years of the depression and chiefly during the war years of 1940-1945. The new movement had a specific character, due to the nature of the city and its job markets. It was, for one thing, predominantly affiliated with the American Federation of Labor. There are several reasons for this. The labor force is disproportionately concentrated in the white collar, service worker and skilled craftsman jobs and these are historically most easily organized by craft type unions. Then too, the AFL had a more "conservative" reputation and when an open shop was organized it was frequently preferred by both workers and management to the more "radical" CIO. Finally, Los Angeles, thinly settled and sprawling, is extremely dependent upon local transport; the trucks are the very carriers of life for industry and business. The truck drivers were early organized by the AFL Teamsters union and their support became a powerful organizational aid for other unions--generally AFL.

At the same time, heavy industry was relatively less important in Los Angeles before the war and it is to heavy industry and its masses of semi-skilled workers that the CIO appealed most strongly. When heavy industry did begin to move into the area with the beginning of the war boom, the craft complexes of the AFL were already strong and were able to use their local organization and their leverage with employers to facilitate the spread of AFL industrial unions. The International Association of Machinists, originally a craft union, became an important industrial union in aircraft manufacturing; the International Brotherhood of Electrical Workers, another craft union originally, organized many of the large electronics firms.

The AFL did not, of course, completely monopolize heavy industry; the CIO came, from 1937 on, capturing such industries as large-scale meat packing, the big rubber plants, a number of aircraft plants and the shipyards. However, much of its membership came during the war as a result of the "no-strike agreement and a union shop" formula. Many members joined the union because they could not get jobs in war work otherwise; they were, in effect, conscript union men. Having neither struggled for their unions nor lived through major strikes they were precipitated into a mature union organization before they had ever experienced the struggles and growing pains characteristic of such movements as those in Detroit or Akron. Furthermore, many were antagonistic to unions and most were migrants, with few roots in the local community

Thus CIO and AFL alike were, in their local origins, largely the result of the wartime labor shortage and the general conditions of this wartime growth tended both to increase the size of the local unions and to "water the stock" of the movement. Although the memberships are impressive in size the actual degree of solidarity is largely unknown. The Los Angeles labor movement in 1950 might be described as a giant, whose bulk is obvious but whose effective strength remains to be determined. It is a prosperous movement, however, one that has risen from the dead and today controls a substantial part of the work force in the third largest urban complex in the United States.

THE MINORITY SHARE IN UNION MEMBERSHIP*

The job market was "tight" in Los Angeles in 1950. There had been severe cutbacks in the production of aircraft, and shipbuilding was at a near standstill. The many new industries (chiefly smaller firms) which had absorbed part of the wartime labor force were inadequate for the hundreds of thousands who had been gradually released. Unemployment, in March of 1950, was 178,000 for the County, or ten per cent of the total civilian labor force (24). Jobs were a problem and, as always, particularly so for the marginal and less desirable workers. Mexicans, Negroes, and other ethnic workers made up a majority in the long lines before the windows at the State Employment Service offices. Those jobs available to ethnic workers in 1950 were apt to be filled quickly.

At this time, under conditions of a mild recession, twenty-eight International Unions having substantial membership in the County were surveyed. These organizations included over 200,000 members or approximately forty per cent of the local union membership. They were so chosen as to include a disproportionately large part of the ethnic union members; none had discrimnatory clauses in their constitution and they were the internationals singled out by regional officers of the AFL and CIO as containing large proportions of Mexicans, Negroes and other ethnic minorities. The purpose of studying these unions was to gain some notion of the number and location of ethnic union members in the County, to find their relative importance for different unions and the relative importance of different unions for them. Further, through choosing only

* For detailed presentation of the data summarized in this and following chapters, see Greer (16).

unions whose formal policy favored their inclusion it was possible to investigate other reasons for variations in ethnic jobs and union membership observed.

Sixteen of the International Unions were affiliates of the American Federation of Labor. Ten were members of the Congress of Industrial Organizations. Two internationals had been members of CIO but had left the Congress.

Such a sample as this included most of the important unions in CIO having substantial membership in Los Angeles. It neglected several important AFL internationals, reported to be extremely exclusionist, because the unions chosen were those in which ethnic participation is at a maximum.

There are extreme differences in the proportion of Mexicans and Negroes in the various unions; the range is from less than one per cent for both populations combined to over seventy per cent. Since this reflects neither a scarcity of Mexican and Negro workers nor exclusion by the union (nor a refusal of ethnic workers to join unions, for they are chiefly union shops) it is important to assay other causes. One possible factor producing these variations is the federation to which the internationals belonged-- AFL or CIO.

The dichotomy of unions by organizational affiliation is common, and commonly implies a distinct judgement of the two types of union. The CIO was considered to be more liberal and the AFL more conservative. This was born out by union propaganda, speeches and, sometimes, political endorsements. Such ideological differences were frequently thought to determine policy towards the inclusion of ethnic workers in the union membership. When, however, the twenty-eight internationals were divided by federation the results were not at all clear. Both the AFL and the CIO included unions with great variations in their combined Mexican-Negro membership-- from less than five per cent to over sixty-five per cent. The only clear difference is at the extremes; forty-three per cent of the AFL unions had less than fifteen per cent from these groups, but only twenty per cent of the CIO unions had this small a proportion. On the other hand, this is true at the other end of the scale; forty-three per cent of the AFL unions had over forty-five per cent of their members from Mexican and Negro workers but only one-fifth of the CIO unions had that many.

A second common dichotomy of unions separates the industrial unions from the craft unions. An industrial union is one which includes the workers in a majority of the industrially related jobs found in a given area of production. A craft union is one which accepts for membership chiefly workers performing a single, specified kind of job. This dichotomy is also thought to distinguish between the inclusive and the exclusive unions. And, when it is applied, there are seen to be definite differences. The most important difference is between the number of unions having less than fifteen per cent Mexican and Negro members combined; half the craft unions have this small a percentage, as against one-eighth of the industrial unions. The median for the craft unions is eleven per cent; for the industrial unions, thirty-four per cent.

Still, many cases remain which are in sharp contrast to the general trend. There are industrial unions whose Mexican and Negro members combined are less than five per cent of the total and craft unions with over seventy-five per cent from these groups. Such negative cases indicate still other bases for exclusion or inclusion of ethnic workers.

In examining these cases attention is called to the tremendous variation, within each category of union, in the nature of the work. In the craft union category the range is from cooks to dishwashers, from clerical workers to janitors, from ornamental plasterers to hodcarriers. This is a range extending from the very bottom to the upper middle of the Edwards socio-economic ranking of occupations (11). On the other hand, the industrial internationals range from those with high percentages of unskilled and semiskilled labor to those, such as the Communications Workers of America (the telephone workers) and the Oil Workers International, with high percentages of skilled craftsmen, clerical and customer service workers. The inclusion of Negroes and Mexicans in the unions seemed directly associated with the kind of work performed by the members.

With this in mind the internationals were reclassified into four broad job levels. The first included customer service and clerical work; the second were the craftsman jobs, and included only those which demand a highly specific skill that can be learned only through application over a long period of time; the third were the industrial operative jobs, including only those who work in large plants, specialized and rationally organized for production; the final category, that of the one-job laborer, includes highly specified work which, basis for union jurisdiction though it is, cannot be considered a craft in the sense denoted above; this includes construction labor, longshore work and the janitorial jobs.

This reclassification (necessitating the division of some internationals into two membership groups) resulted in an extremely sharp and clear distinction between internationals with many Negroes and Mexicans and those with very small contingents. (The internationals, their classification and their ethnic contingents are reported in Table I, Appendix "A"). Those unions with large ethnic proportions are industrial or one-job labor unions; those with few Mexicans or Negroes are in customer service, clerical or craft work (with the single exception of the highly skilled work in the Oil Workers jurisdiction). In these twenty-eight international unions, chosen especially for their large numbers of minority group members, no customer service or clerical workers union has over fourteen per cent of its members from these two populations combined. But all one-job laborer unions have at least one-fourth of their members from Mexican and Negro workers and the average percentage is over fifty.

It must not be supposed that these were federation lines in a new disguise. Two customer service workers unions were CIO, five industrial operative unions were AFL and a one-job union, the Longshoreman's Union, is a disaffiliate of CIO. All craftsman's unions were AFL, however. The pattern crosses federation lines.

The distribution of all Mexican and Negro union members in the sample, relative to that of the total non-Negro/Mexican members, is shown in Table 2-1.

TABLE 2-1

The Distribution of Mexican and Negro Union Members in Four Types of International Unions

TYPE OF UNION	MEMBERS AS A PROPORTION OF ALL		
	MEXICAN MEMBERS	NEGRO MEMBERS	OTHER MEMBERS
Customer Service and Clerical	.05	.04	.20
Craftsman	.10	.03	.10
Industrial Operative	.59	.58	.55
One-job Laborer	.26	.36	.15
	1.00	1.01	1.00

The exclusion of Mexicans and Negroes in the highest job class is very uniform; the range for the Negroes in the customer service workers' unions is from one to five per cent and that for Mexicans is similar. The range is wider and the mean much higher in the industrial workers unions.

Negroes and Mexicans, then, are found included and excluded similarly in the unions of the sample. The Mexican proportion is equal to, or higher than, the Negro proportion in all categories except the one-job unions. This pattern of association is consistent with other studies of these minorities. Shevky found, in his analysis of the social areas of Los Angeles, the same close association between Mexicans and Negroes in their residential distribution, but none between either and the Jewish population (37). From another perspective one may say that they are excluded consistently from the same areas.

In summary: The classification of unions in this sample by job-type proves by far the most effective means of predicting the proportion of Mexicans and Negroes in the membership, regardless of international affiliation or the organizational type (craft or industrial) of the union. All one-job unions have high percentages of Negroes and Mexicans, whether they organize longshoremen or dishwashers; all customer service unions have few if any such members.

The Job Hierarchy and Ethnic Entry:

These categories of jobs, from one-job laborer to customer service, are evidently part of a hierarchy, at least where ethnic exclusion is concerned; yet the nature of the hierarchy is not self-evident. It is certainly not a skill hierarchy. Those who work in the killing operations of the meat packing industry are more highly skilled than the customer service personnel in the Utility Workers Union, yet Negroes dominate the former position and are so scarce in the latter that union officials can call them by name. Nor, on the other hand, is this an income hierarchy. Cement finishers and construction laborers draw higher wages than clerical and service workers in many industries. It is not even a prestige hierarchy; truck drivers, predominantly neither Mexican nor Negroes, have no more prestige than cement finishers, who are very apt to be one or the other.

The hierarchy can provisionally be considered as based on the value of the job to the worker. This value, which cannot be deduced directly from any one aspect of the job, may be considered a general cultural definition. As such, the rank of the job becomes a part of the culture and various jobs fall into an array similar to that inferred by North and Hatt in their study of occupational prestige (28). The rank order of the job is, however, derived from selected aspects of the work itself, and those selected vary from job to job.

Another factor of great importance is employer preference or resistance. It cannot be directly derived from the general social definition, but the two factors are not unrelated. Within the limits of the workers' technical ability to do the job, further barriers to ethnic entry usually coincide with the value of the job to prospective employees in general. If its value is high it will tend to attract the non-ethnic workers; if the employer has any preference it will be for such candidates. Indications are that the two factors coincide in a particularly neat fashion where the work entails customer contact. And here, too, it is frequently impossible to separate the employer's personal preference from his estimate of customer reaction to Negro or Mexican employees.

If, on the other hand, the job has a low value, it will attract fewer candidates from the more highly valued work force and more Negroes and Mexicans; the operation of the employer's preference will be limited and Mexicans or Negroes are apt to be hired. Such are the considerations which seem most crucial in explaining the concentration of Negroes and Mexicans in one-job unions and their exclusion from the customer service unions.

Still it is in just those job levels where Negroes and Mexicans are most scarce, in the craft unions, that union control over the point of entering employment is strongest (through the hiring hall). The exclusion of ethnic workers is thus frequently considered to be a result of craft organization. This hypothesis is contradicted, however, by the scarcity of ethnic workers in customer service and clerical work regardless of union organization, and by their plenitude in the craft-type organizations of the one-job laborers. In view of these data, it seems more accurate to state the relation between craft unions and the entry of ethnics as follows: (A) the basic hiring point is the employer (B) unions exist in an accomodative relation with employers (C) the employer is likely to be especially conscious of color in certain jobs, especially where customer contact is involved (D) non-ethnic workers will be available for these jobs and he will hire them and, (E), such jobs when organized are likely to be in a craft union's jurisdiction.

Of course the extremely exclusionist union with great strike power can effect a color line, However, it must be remembered that the International Unions in this sample were especially chosen because they were not exclusionist. The scarcity of Negroes and Mexicans in customer service unions must be related to the general scarcity of job opportunities for them in retail sales, clerical work and service work catering to the general population. It seems highly probable, on the basis of this data, that the relative exclusion of Mexicans and Negroes from unions at certain job-levels is more clearly the result of hiring practices in industry than of the ethnic policy of the unions.

If the minority is already a large part of the union's membership the situation is quite different. When this does occur, however, it can usually be traced to the initiative of the employer, not the union. As one business agent of a large craft union put it: "The Negro fellows weren't in this union until the war, about 1943. They're local guys, who were non-union before that. When we couldn't get men, we had to let the contractors hire whoever they could."

The chief agency of change in the ethnic composition of the unions is the supply and character of labor in relation to effective demand. Once men are working the union must organize them, no matter what their ethnic identification.

The Natural History of Ethnic Entry into the Unions:

The above propositions are born out by the difference in the distribution of the Negro and Mexican union members at different job-levels in these internationals. (see above, Table 2-1). Although there are similarities, the Mexican distribution is nearer that of the non-Mexican/Negro distribution than is that of the Negroes. This is largely due to their greater concentration in the craft unions of the building trades, and this in turn is due to their earlier entry into the job market and hence the union.

The Mexicans held this advantage in nearly all of the unions in this sample. Of the internationals with significant proportions of members who were Mexican (nineteen in all) eighty per cent found the Mexicans an important part of the work force in the industry at the time the union started its organizing drive. In the others, Mexicans entered the industry shortly after the first union organizing.

The Mexican workers are largely native and, where they are migrants, are usually old migrants from the 1920's. They entered Los Angeles industry early and soon became important parts of the workforce in such crafts as cement finishing and painting and such industries as meat packing and steel working. They were for the most part non-union. When, however, the wave of industrial unionism reached Los Angeles in the late 1930's and early 1940's, they became members of the industrial unions which, in many cases, would have failed without them.

Negroes are a newer contingent in all cases. The wartime labor shortage is almost universally responsible for their entry into the different work forces and unions studied. Whether the shortage caused the employment of local Negroes, hitherto excluded, or encouraged Negro workers to come to Los Angeles, the date of entry is between 1940 and 1947 for all but the Retail Clerks, the packinghouse unions, and the Building Laborers. A very large proportion are wartime migrants, principally from the South, the Midwest and the Southwest; they migrated into the region, the industry and the union, particularly the unions organizing those industries most affected by the wartime shortage. The Mexicans, in contrast, already held a foothold in most of these industries; with the war, that hold was extended and secured.

War industry drained manpower, first from other industries, then from the excluded groups. As this occurred, Negroes and Mexicans became dispersed throughout much of the job structure. There was a flow of non-ethnic workers out of the "dirty work" into the more highly valued jobs in aircraft and ship building; the flow of Mexican and Negro labor filled the empty jobs left behind and moved as far as semiskilled jobs in aircraft and ship building during the extreme labor shortage. This was generally the high-water mark. Then, as the shortage was reduced with the loss of war contracts, the flow was reversed, and they had difficulty in keeping their positions even in the "dirty jobs." An official in a union organizing heavy labor put it this way.

> "The Negroes were in heavy industry before 1941, but really they went in just before Pearl Harbor. I'd say the white people in the foundries at that time sought shipbuilding jobs, and the way was not yet open for Negroes. After the war the Negroes who had been in aircraft and shipbuilding came back to the foundries and accumulated seniority to protect their jobs. Those displaced Negroes had been replaced by older men who were about through anyway... The same thing holds for rubber-- the seniority from the war is all that's holding them and when they lose it they're out of luck."

It is notable that in the industrial unions Negroes and Mexicans had accumulated seniority and stayed, for almost thirty per cent of the members of those industrial unions studied were Negroes or Mexicans.

The ebb-tide was stronger in customer service and clerical jobs, where seniority clauses are apt to be less effective. The following is the report of an interview with the business agent of a customer service local union.

> "Mr. X offered the information that the large numbers of Negroes still in the industry was dependent on the fact that it had been necessary to scrape the bottom of the barrel during the war. He stated that, according to his observations, the three largest operators in his jurisdiction were trying to rid themselves as fast as possible of their Negro employees. This was being done through laying them off and failing to

> rehire when more workers were again needed. Both business agents explained there was no seniority clause affecting hiring or firing until recently."

In summary, the high percentage of Negroes and Mexicans in the industrial internationals can thus be explained by the extremely large demand for mass labor during the war and their availability at the time; their persistence is due to union job protection and the disvalued nature of much of the work. In the customer service labor market, in contrast, there was less demand during the shortage and less protection for them afterwards; most wartime gains were wiped out.

The difference in the distribution of the two populations is a result of the earlier entrance of Mexicans into the various labor forces, as well as their larger numbers in the County. The later arrival of the Negroes and their movement into industrial work explains both their weakness in the craft jobs and their importance in the industrial work force. (Their lower position in the "ethnic pecking order" probably constitutes an additional handicap for them, though it is difficult to weigh it under the circumstances.) Both ethnic populations were disproportionately concentrated in the one-job unions, but the Negroes much more so than the Mexicans; by 1950 four out of each ten Negro union members studied were in the bottom of the job hierarchy.

In these International Unions, formal policy and the attitudes of individual officers toward the inclusion of Mexicans and Negroes was either favorable or *laissez faire*. There seemed to be no instance of ethnic exclusion which could be considered a direct result of union policy. On the other hand, no case was observed where an extension of job opportunities could be considered due to union policy. Only in protecting seniority did the unions have an effect on labor market composition. The leaders of several unions in the industrial and one-job categories (AFL, CIO and disaffiliates) indicated a personal desire to change the pattern, but confessed their inability to do so. And, where the pattern had changed, it had changed by employer initiative, which in turn was due to a tight labor market. It is unlikely that any union *could* have increased the proportions of Mexicans and Negroes hired during the depression and it is equally unlikely that unions could have prevented the great increase of these populations in Los Angeles industry during the war years. Once these populations became significant parts of the various jurisdictions, however, the unions could and did organize them.

TWENTY-ONE LOCAL UNIONS AND THEIR MINORITY MEMBERS

From the International Unions discussed, twenty-one locals were selected for more intense study. Here the subject of study is a group of concrete organizations, spatially centered--face to face collectives. These locals constitute a wide range of types, whether judged by the socio-economic level of the jobs, size of the membership, function of the union, political character of the union in its internal affairs and foreign relations, or almost any other important criterion. The variety and range of the locals allows some control over hasty generalizations, yet makes possible a comparative case study with detailed inquiry at selected points.

Information concerning these locals falls into two classes centered, respectively, around the job and the union hall. At the first level important data concern the size of the labor force in the union jurisdiction, job-level of the membership, ethnic composition of the local and ethnic job-levels. The second class of data concerns the political participation of the members in the locals. This chapter is devoted to a description of participation in the work force; in following chapters the union will be described as a formal organization.

The sample of local unions included thirteen AFL locals, six CIO and two ex-CIO organizations; they were locals having among the highest proportions of ethnic members in the County. The preponderance of AFL locals is due to two considerations. First, the AFL was the dominant federation in Los Angeles County, with approximately four-fifths of the members and, second, the AFL included a much wider range of job types and union organizational types than did the CIO. For both empirical and theoretical reasons a wider sample of AFL locals seemed more useful. The locals, their membership, and their ethnic proportions, are described in Table II, Appendix "A".

The Distributions of Mexican and Negro Members in the Locals:

The twenty-one locals have a total membership of some 60,000-- approximately one-eighth of the union members in Los Angeles County. They are exceptionally heavily weighted with members from ethnic minorities; half of the membership is made up of Mexicans, Negroes, Jews, Italians, Japanese and Russians. (See Table II, Appendix "A".) Such a sample, unrepresentative in the extreme of all locals in the County, may be considered a fair sample of those with large concentrations of ethnic members. If quantitative strength in the membership allows for fuller union citizenship, these locals should register the high water mark of ethnic participation in the local labor movement.

Of 30,000 ethnic members, forty-five per cent are Mexican, thirty-seven per cent Negro and another eighteen per cent are Jews, Japanese, Italians, and Russian Molokans in that order of importance. Since this sample of locals is far from random it is impossible to generalize concerning the distribution of the smaller and less visible ethnic minorities. The greater their concentration, the greater room there is for error through omission in a small sample of locals.

Approximately two-thirds of the locals have a combined Mexican and Negro membership of forty-five per cent or more. This includes one craftsmans' local, nine industrial locals, and all one-job locals. Mexicans and Negroes are a majority in locals organizing janitor work, construction labor, meat packing, garment work, the brick and clay industry, the furniture industry and cement finishing. With the exception of the furniture industry these are jobs in which hard, dirty work predominates; the furniture industry is, as noted earlier, a recently developed industry in the local area and it constitutes an impressive example of the way in which an ethnic minority (the Mexicans) can move rapidly upward in job-levels with the expansion of new industry. Mexicans predominate in many plants and are heavily distributed throughout job levels.

Dividing the locals into three categories by job-level of the local, the mean percentage of Mexican and Negro members combined in each type, and the range of percentages in the type, are as follows.

TABLE 2-2

Mean Proportion and Range of Mexican and Negro Members Combined in the Locals

JOB LEVEL	MEXICANS MEAN	MEXICANS RANGE	NEGROES MEAN	NEGROES RANGE	MEXICANS & NEGROES MEAN	MEXICANS & NEGROES RANGE
Craft and Customer Service (5)	.18	.07-.50	.07	.00-.20	.22	.10-.70
Industrial (13)	.35	.12-.50	.16	.03-.38	.52	.25-.88
One-job (3)	.16	.02-.37	.46	.39-.50	..62	.50-.76

The importance of the Mexican and Negro contingents in the industrial locals is clear when it is noted that, except for the small Shipyards Workers' Local, all have thirty per cent or more of their members from these populations. Mexicans are under ten per cent of the members in only two locals; Negroes, however, are less than ten per cent in eight locals. These include all locals above the industrial workers level except the Cement Finishers' Local. Negroes are the largest ethnic population in all three one-job locals.

As is true for the total membership of the International Unions in the County, Mexicans and Negroes are closely associated both in and out of these local unions. In the one local where exclusion of Negroes is found, the Mexican share of the membership is small (ten per cent). Any local with a large number of one ethnic minority is apt to have a significant number of the other.

Mexicans, however, as in the international memberships as a whole, have a larger proportional share of the better jobs. Negroes are as common as Mexicans only in the one-job unions, in meat packing and in the Mine, Mill and Smelter Workers' Local's jurisdiction. They are the majority group only in the janitor workers' unions. In this sample of local unions, to summarize, two-thirds of all Negro union members were in the one-job laborer locals; two-thirds of all Mexican members were in the industrial locals.

Relative Job Levels of Mexicans and Negroes:

An index of relative job level of Mexicans or Negroes in any given industrial union membership was computed by taking their weighted average job-level (weighting unskilled, semi-skilled, and skilled jobs as one, two, and three) as a percentage of that for the non-Negro/Mexican membership. If jobs are equally available to Mexicans, for example, their weighted job-level should be that of the non-ethnic membership; if they have an advantage it should be higher, if a disability, lower.

The Mexican job level is equal to, or higher than, that of the non-ethnic members in ten out of thirteen industrial locals. The Negro job-levels are as high in seven. The average index for Negro job-levels (unweighted by the size of the locals) is minus six per cent, while the average for Mexicans is plus seven per cent. However, though the Negro job-level is usually lower than that of Mexican workers, there is an association; where Mexican job-levels are high, Negro job-levels are also relatively high, and *vice versa*. The association between Mexican and Negro workers in their entry to a labor force holds also for their entry into specific job-levels within the industry.

Likewise, the initial advantage of the Mexican workers carries over. Mexicans have been important segments of the labor force since before the origin of the local in nine of the thirteen unions. Negroes, on the other hand, were important before Pearl Harbor only in the meat packing industry. Here they were an established part of the work force to be organized, and here they have an average job-level higher than that for the total non-Negro/Mexican membership.

The advantage of earlier entry, which results in a larger proportion of Mexican workers in these union memberships, also affects the average job-level of Mexicans. The numerical strength of Mexicans or Negroes in an industrial workforce is directly related to their job level. The following summary table indicates the strength of this relationship.

TABLE 2-3

Association Between Proportion of Minority in a Membership And Index of Minority Job-level: 13 Locals

PROPORTION OF TOTAL MEMBERS	INDEX OF JOB-LEVEL FOR THE MINORITY					
	-.49 to -.30	-.29 to -.10	-.09 to + 9	+10 to + 29	+30 to +49	+50 to +69
.00 to .11	2	-	2	-	-	-
.11 to .30	1	1	4	-	-	1
.31 to .40	-	-	2	-	- -	-
.41 to .50	-	2	2	1	2	-

None of the ethnic contingents amounting to less than one-fifth of the membership have a job level above average and, in the thirteen cases where Negro or Mexican contingents were one-fifth or more of the total membership, only four had a job-level below average.

Such an association is not surprising for, given an inflexible ratio between skilled, semiskilled and unskilled jobs, it is simply not possible to hire Mexicans or Negroes beyond a certain number without upgrading them. This rough relationship is, however, fundamental to any consideration of the upward mobility of ethnic minorities; if the employment practices at the factory gate are non-discrimnatory, the ethnic workers must eventually reach job-levels equal to those of other workers.

This relationship between quantity and quality of jobs is based upon all Mexican and Negro contingents in the industrial locals. The majority of the small ethnic contingents with low job-levels is Negro however, while Mexican contingents are usually between forty-one and fifty per cent of the total members. This difference between the two groups does not, however, account for the association between quantity and quality of jobs; it holds for each ethnic population when considered separately.

THE CRAFT-INDUSTRIAL DICHOTOMY AND MINORITY JOBS

When the plant gate is first opened to Mexicans or Negroes they enter in a menial capacity, as sweepers or unskilled laborers. If they remain a small part of the work force they are apt to keep to these low level jobs. The union seniority is ordinarily good only for the department in which the worker is employed and there are powerful resistances to any broader base. When departmental seniority coincides with a union policy of "protecting minority jobs for minority"guys" it tends to structure the situation so as to admit a small, segregated population of ethnic workers to the job and the union. This pattern is common for Negroes and holds for Mexicans in some industries; it is a quota system of hiring. It prevents dispersion of ethnic workers throughout the industry and it cannot survive non-discrimnatory hiring practices.

When, however, there are large increases in employment opportunities for ethnic workers, such as those brought about in Los Angeles by the wartime labor shortage, it is in the industrially organized work that the greatest dispersion of these workers through the entire job hierarchy will occur. This is due in part to the differences in jobs typically organized by craft-type unions; it is also the result of union structure. For, insofar as a given pattern of ethnic exclusion is the result of mutual commitments and mutually reinforcing norms of organized groups, the fewer the organizations committed to that pattern the more rapidly can change proceed.

In the labor force fragmented by craft unionism (including craft unions for those without a craft, the unskilled) there are many opportunities for vested interests in exclusion to develop, since there is a specialized union for each job category and since each union leadership group is dependent upon the present incumbents of the job for its own strength. The organizational complex tends to protect desirable jobs by limiting new recruits to the low-level work. Upgrading is proportionally more difficult for Mexican or Negro workers, since it requires organizational as well as occupational mobility. In the industrially organized complex of jobs one union controls all job levels and Mexican or Negroes at the lowest job-level are constituents of that union.

The entering point is the same in both craft-complex and industrially organized work; ethnic minorities come in at the lowest level. The chief difference that is apparent is in their relative job-level once they are established. Although the proportion of the total work-force made up of Mexicans and Negroes was very similar in the craft-type International Unions studied and in this sample of thirteen industrial locals, their relative job-levels were very dissimilar.

If the craft-type internationals are classified by job-level into skilled workers (such as cooks and carpenters), semi-skilled workers (such as truck drivers and waitresses) and unskilled workers (such as longshoremen and dishwashers) the average job-level of Mexicans and Negroes can be compared with that of the remaining members of the unions. This relative job-level may then be compared with their relative level in the industrial internationals, and the likelihood of upward job mobility in the two kinds of unions can be examined.

In the craft-type International Union membership the weighted job-level for all Mexicans is twelve per cent below average for the non-Mexican/Negro union members; for all Negro members, it is forty per cent below the average of these other members. These differences indicate a powerful tendency for craft-type organization to concentrate these groups in the unskilled jobs. In contrast, the weighted job-levels for all Mexicans in the industrial locals is three per cent above average and that for Negroes is one per cent above average. For Negroes and Mexicans in these industrial locals as a whole, the probability of attaining a given job level is exactly the same as that for the non-Negro/Mexican workers.

These differences are sharp and clear. While the sample is not random, these craft-organized unions include over 50,000 workers and forty-five per cent are Mexican or Negro. They were chosen for their high proportions of ethnic members and the job-levels of their Mexican and Negro members are compared only with those of non-Mexican/Negro workers in the same unions.

The chief difference, then, in the position of ethnic minorities in this sample of craft-type unions and in the industrial locals is not one of the quantity of job opportunities, but rather a difference in the quality of jobs available to them. In the industrial locals the average job-levels are similar for Mexican, Negro and other members, but in the craft-organized work forces, in which each job-level is organized by a separate union, Mexicans and Negroes are apt to remain in unskilled labor jobs until they saturate the local unions involved, without ever moving to the next step above--even though that step is only to a job as a stock clerk or a truck driver.

A SUMMARY STATEMENT

Mexican and Negro workers, attracted to Los Angeles by the expansion of economic opportunity, were important parts of the labor force by 1950. At that time, under the conditions of a mild recession, twenty-eight International Unions in the County with very large contingents of these minorities in their membership were studied. The distribution of Mexican and Negro workers followed a pattern in which the usual level of the jobs organized by the union was a major determinant of their inclusion or exclusion. Few of them worked in customer service or clerical jobs; more worked as craftsmen; a very large proportion worked in those jobs organized by industrial unions; they were a majority of the members in the one-job laborer unions.

Employer hiring practices and union cooperation with the employer constituted barriers to the more desirable jobs; this funnelled Mexican and Negro workers into the industrial and one-job unions. With the wartime labor shortage this occurred at an extremely rapid rate. Mexicans, chiefly a native population, had already gained a foothold in many industries and dominated others (chiefly the heavy industries and the "dirty" jobs); the war spread them throughout the jobs hierarchies and into new fields. Negroes, who entered most industries only in the 1940's as a consequence of the war, followed the same paths and are found associated with Mexicans in all but a very few of the union work forces studied.

In the twenty-one locals the same pattern of concentration by the job-level of the membership occurred. Mexicans, however, had a higher concentration in the craftsmans unions and were fewer than Negroes in the one-job laborer locals.

This was consistent with the relative job-levels of the two minorities within the industrial locals. Mexicans had a higher average job-level than Negroes in all but a few unions and Negroes were markedly favored only in the Packinghouse Workers' locals. The advantage of earlier entrance was evident in the Mexican job-distribution and, for the Negroes, in the packinghouse unions. However, in work organized through craft-union complexes both Mexicans and Negroes have very low job-levels; their date of entry makes little difference. They are apt to be largely confined to the unskilled jobs. The dispersion of Negroes and Mexicans throughout a job hierarchy is apparently much easier when workers are organized by industrial locals. The difference is not necessarily one of getting jobs-- it is a difference in the ability to move from a lower job-level to a higher one.

The integration of an ethnic minority in an urban labor force moves through these steps. First there is an expansion of job opportunities beyond the ability of the "preferred," non-ethnic labor force to fill them, followed by the recruitment of ethnic workers. These workers enter at the lower levels and, if the union-management barriers hold, are segregated there-- a small and constant part of the workforce. If, however, the work is organized by industrial unions and the labor shortage continues the management resistance is likely to disappear, and ethnic workers will continue to increase until they are necessarily upgraded. Since there is a normal job scarcity for ethnic workers, they will soon become a major part of the workforce and when this occurs their job-levels will be comparable to those of non-ethnic workers.

In Los Angeles the Mexican workers have gone through this entire process in a number of union work forces studied. This is clearly illustrated in the Furniture Workers Union, at that time CIO (as well as in the AFL and Independent locals), in the Packinghouse Workers (both those formerly AFL and CIO) and in the Steelworkers Local. They are in process of reaching full job-parity in the garment industry, the utilities industry and the metals industries, particularly heavy metals. In all of these industries, however, they have been a major part of the labor force for the past twenty years or longer. Negroes are a more recent contingent in almost all cases; they are still numerically unimportant in many of the unions studied and their job-levels frequently reflect a small contingent of functionally segregated workers. Thus in the Steelworkers' Local's membership they are found only in two plants and in one, only as sweepers. In the Furniture Workers (Ind.) they are preponderantly concentrated in one large firm at unskilled labor. In the packinghouse workers' unions, however, are Negroes with a long local history in the work force, and the process is nearing completion; they are almost integrated,

Integration begins as a result of the play of the market, in which these workers are unknown quantities or "damaged goods." They are used by marginal establishments, including those industries just organizing in the locality. With a shortage, however, they are more widely acceptable and may rapidly become a necessary condition for production. Increasing in numbers within a unionized industry they reach job-parity and, at the same time, take out their citizenship papers in the union. When this occurs, the play of the market is modified by the organizational power of the union.

CHAPTER III

ETHNIC PARTICIPATION AND REPRESENTATION

Attendance at Meetings

The local union is always the unit of membership. It is here that the members belong to the union and here that the union is exposed to its members. Membership in the international is indirect, through the local. At the level of the locals, the labor movement may be observed in the behavior of given, concrete social groups.

The points at which rank and file participation is possible are as follows; (1) in some locals the members meet as a plant unit to consider issues, select plantwide officers and, in some cases, elect executive board members for the executive board of the larger organization (2) the total membership of the local meets to consider routine business and (3) the total membership of the local meets periodically to elect the "local-wide" officers, vote on contracts and consider strike action. The first type of meeting will be called "Plant Unit meetings," the second, "General Membership meetings" and the third, "Special Election meetings."

The routing meetings are usually monthly and are conducted in the terms of parliamentary procedure; their etiquette is derived from _Robert's Rules of Order_. The associational form of the local union is, thus, one common to voluntary associations in America. The amount of membership participation in the various types of meetings will be described, followed by an analysis of leadership groups.

Participation in Plant Unit Meetings:

Plant Unit meetings occur only in the industrial locals of the sample. In six locals they are held regularly, having many of the functions for the plant group which the General Membership meeting has for the local as a whole; in the other locals they are held only when specific issues arise that concern the plant membership. A high rate of attendance is usual at those locals which have shop meetings only for a crisis. More important, however, is the high attendance in those locals which have routine monthly Plant Unit meetings. The average for these is over one-half the members, ranging from nearly 100 per cent to fifteen per cent. This average is five times the usual attendance for the General Membership meetings.

The most obvious reason for the difference is the spatial

location of the members; a large local usually has a membership scattered over the entire County and the difficulties of transportation to the meetings act as a sieve, through which only the more powerfully motivated members penetrate. They are few in number, even when they are joined by those who happen to live near the union hall. Plant Unit meetings, in contrast, can be held immediately after the work shift is finished, when all members are near the meeting place.

Such is the reason most frequently inferred by union leaders for the high attendance at Plant Unit meetings and it undoubtedly has validity. It seems likely, however, that higher attendance is also due to the greater homogeneity of interest among the members from a single plant. The immediacy of the shared problems which they confront is apparent; the common enemy is at hand and is well known to all and the common leader is also well known. The meetings occur within the context of many and varied personal associations resulting from on-the-job interaction. In short, the union organization at this level is reinforced by work associations and tends towards "community." Insofar as this is true various informal sanctions operate on the individual member, reinforcing the meaning of his more abstract committments as a good union man and requiring his attendance at the meetings.

There is more rank and file participation in these meetings than at any other level of the union structure. The general pattern of attendance is one in which older and more highly skilled workers attend most frequently and regularly. Negroes and Mexicans attend, not in proportion to their total numbers in the plant, but to their numbers in the higher job levels. This indicates that the organizational backbone of these industrial locals may be found in the skilled and more responsible jobs--an impression to be tested later.

The Nature of General Membership Meetings:

The routine General Membership meeting is important as a source of information and influence, and for purposes of this analysis, as an indicator of interest in the union organization. Certain questions arise concerning the composition of these meetings-- who comes, why they come, what they do. A definitive answer is not possible on the basis of this data but certain tendencies are apparent.

In one of the smaller locals, the Packinghouse Workers CIO, some forty-five members usually attended the meetings, from a total membership of 260 persons. In the words of their president:

"Well, out of forty-five people, they would split into about six or eight white guys, the drivers and the rest. No, on second thought you wouldn't get that many drivers unless you had a situation where they knew something was up, then you'd get most of them out.
Then you'd get about six or seven plant Negroes and about six people from your executive board, about half the board, the important ones-- that is, president, secretary, treasurer and the sargeant-at-arms--they would always be there.
Then you'd get the guys who came sorta because they wanted to kill time, guys who get drunk and sit quietly and say nothing-- you'd get about ten or twelve of them, mostly Negroes, maybe one or two Mexicans. No whites, All ages, a wide span from very young to older people.
Then, finally, you'd get a few people with individual beefs. Come to think of it, on individual beefs, I don't remember ever seeing anyone come but Mexicans and Negroes. This group would fluctuate, of course."
Question: Would any other specific groups besides the drivers come out for an issue?
"No, you wouldn't get none on an issue except the drivers who are fairly well organized. Generally, nobody knows about an issue until the meeting."

In a small craft local the General Membership meetings are described as follows.

"The average meeting? Well, about fifty guys out of 400 members. Some of them because they want to get out in the evening, and some because they're really curious about knowing what's going on. The rest have special beefs. A big percentage is the same at every meeting. Yeah, you would call these the "actives", the "regulars"- you see, they are the guys you usually see at a meeting."

Teamster Local #1 has the largest proportion attending the General Membership meeting of any larger local; it is described by a rank and file active.

"You know, I was surprised at the number of guys that come out to those meetings. I'd say 250 to 300 every time. Why? Oh, to get out with the boys and get drunk, to talk shop, and so on. But you know, there's also a

lot of loyalty to an organization that's about the only one most of them belong to. They work on a truck or maybe a dock, alone, busy as hell all day, working as atomized units without any chance to talk to other guys about the work.
Why, I've sat next to teamsters at parties and heard them talk in great detail about their work. How they loaded this stuff or drove that. I've heard a guy go on for hours about how fast he loaded how much freight and the methods he used and so on. And how to drive a truck--the subject is just inexhaustible! Their identification with their jobs is pretty damned high."

The business agent of the local volunteered identical information, emphasizing the excuse "to get away from home and get drunk." It must be noted that there is no rank-and-file participation in the power structure of this local. Meetings were described by the active quoted above as chiefly "speech making by the hired officers."

The business agent of the Cement Finishers gives the following rather lively picture of his local's participation.

"We used to notify everyone and got sixty-five to come, out of over 800 members. The ten per cent that came were all rabble-- the ordinary guys wouldn't come. (Why not?) There was hecklin' and sluggin'-- and so many guys carried knives-- colored guys. We had cutting scrapes right here in the union hall. One guy even took a jab at me."
(Question: What about-- what did they do?)
"They'd accuse the business agent of false charges. There was no order in the meetings and you couldn't fine them-- you had to have a vote of the membership to do that, and they was the only members who would come. Meetings would just get out of hand-- we couldn't elect officers or anything. We had about a dozen Communist Party members too, and that didn't help. The local finally went into receivership it got so bad; we haven't had a real election in two years."

The business agent of the Utility Workers local, in considering the low degree of participation at the meetings, finally made the following summary statement: "You can't get 'em interested."

"You can't get the membership interested in technical union affairs. They don't give a damn. They figure that we represent them and that they pay us to do it and so what the Hell!"

This statement in one or another form recurred throughout the course of the study.

The small groups attending General Membership meetings are, then, fairly stable but highly differentiated internally. One important distinction is between the regulars and those who come for a "special beef." The regulars seem to be constant in size (though there is probably a musical chairs turnover in composition) while the latter group fluctuates. Within the regulars two broad classes may be distinguished; those who come for union activity and those who come "because they have nothing better to do"-- for "social" reasons. The union participants included stewards and officers and a residue of actives without office. The irregulars fall into those interested in an issue and those who wish to communicate their personal problem to the officers.

The meetings are largely ritual; elected officers sit on the rostrum, the minutes of the last meeting are read, deliberations of the board (in edited form) are presented, new members initiated, minor issues raised and acted upon and the paid staff reports. The pattern is one common to voluntary organizations. If there is no opposition all goes quietly, until adjournment. After this, those who are out for a social evening drink and talk shop in the nearest bar. However, as the business agent of the Cement Finishers remarked, an opposition can cause considerable excitement. The General Membership meeting, with its low attendance and self-selected population, is extremely vulnerable to what one leader described as "the politically over-alert."

Functions of the Meetings:

Although the interest of most members is not strong enough to bring them out to these meetings, there is usually some communication from those present to the other members. This occurs on the job, in work association.

> "The members know; they find out what's going on. You see, they go to the guys who come down and they say, 'Hey, you went to the meeting last night, what the hell's going on?' And they find out. So the word gets around. The meetings serve their purpose alright. Its on the jobs that they find out what's up."

General Membership meetings serve as communication channels, directly to the active members, indirectly to those who stay away. The communication is, notably, <u>one-way</u> to the latter group; they have no opportunity to talk back.

The meetings serve another function. Although actual decisions made here are usually of lesser importance than those made in the Special Election meetings, these meetings are still organizational arenas and in them "spokesmen" arise. The regular meetings are the lowest levels at which the individual member has much of a chance to be heard by the "localwide" membership. A certain amount of influence can be generated here, both through the members and through proximity to the executive board and staff.

The spokesman, if he is so accepted by a few members, then has a primitive organization or following and any such subgroup can exert pressure on the officers. This may not produce friendship or sponsorship; the business agent of one local, describing his lone Mexican officer, called him a "rabble rouser" --but the Mexican was on the "localwide" level of leadership and had influence. The small turnout at these meetings gives, to the vocal minority, a disproportionate weight. To quote one leader:

> "Your little group may have nothing but their own convictions and their own votes, but you know, the members begin to listen and respect them. The leaders have to take account of them. They may <u>never</u> get the members to vote for them, but they influence policy all the same. You see this very clearly when you compare the unions where there are no such spokesmen."

In this view, the relative attendance of Mexicans and Negroes at General Membership meetings has an importance out of proportion to the importance of the decisions made here. Locals where ethnic contingents participate intensely should be locals whose staff is very sensitive to ethnic issues. And, in such locals, ethnic leadership should be relatively easy.

General Membership meetings, then, function as means of communication and constitute the arenas where spokesmen arise. They attract a small but important segment of the membership.

Size, Space, and Participation:

Studies of local unions have consistently reported very low attendance figures for the routine meetings. The present study, though probably biased in favor of high participation, does little to dispel previous conclusions. The average attendance of the entire membership at routine meetings in these locals is slightly over eleven per cent, ranging from less than two per cent to forty-four per cent. The modal percentage of members attending is under ten. (Attendance rates, with relative attendance of ethnic members, are presented in Table III, Appendix "A".)

The difference in attendance between industrial and craft-type locals is particularly striking; it is twice as high in the former. On further analysis, however, this can be accounted for by difference in size between the two types of locals. Of nine locals with less than ten per cent attending, none has a membership of less than 1,000, and the average is 3,500 members. Of the eight locals whose attendance ranges from eleven to forty-four per cent, however, only three have more than 1,000 members-- and each of these has recently been split by raids from an employer's association or another union. Omitting these locals in very atypical states of activity, the remaining fourteen locals vary sharply in attendance by size. Those with more than ten per cent attending have average memberships of only 400.

When the absolute number of members who attend General Membership meetings is considered the range is from forty-five to 550 members. The mean number attending is 143. Two-thirds of these twenty-one locals usually have no more than 100 members at their routine meetings. Again, the size of the local's membership is important; when the local has an attendance of over 100 members it is a large local. All five of the smaller locals have a usual attendance of less than 100; of the larger ones, five have 100 or less, three have between 100 and 300 and three have between 300 and 800 in attendance. This is, however, weak evidence of any consistent increase in attendance with the size of the local's membership; seven-eighths of these locals have groups in their General Membership meetings that range in size from fifty to 250 members.

In the five smaller locals a distinctly homogeneous kind of membership is involved in each case, whether in work place and industry (for the industrial locals) or geographical area and operation (for the craft type unions). In these cases communication on the job and shared interests can be expected to reinforce attention to the affairs of the local.

Thus the higher percentage participating in smaller locals indicates a point of diminishing returns, at about 250 members attending, regardless of the size of the total membership. The same principle which clarifies the remarkably high attendance at Plant Unit meetings may be applied in reverse to these data. The increase in the size of a local is almost always accompanied by an increase in the spatial, organizational and technological dispersion of the members. The amalgamation of many diverse work groups in a large local will, unless properly taken into account, result in an attenuation of the organizational bonds excepting for the monthly assemblies. These will then suffer from the lack of supporting channels of communication; their attendance will decline in turn.

Consideration of the problems which face the leaders of

large locals, whose members are scattered in small groups over all of Los Angeles County, strengthens this notion.

> "You take something like our local--how in hell can you get people out? They live all over L. A. The Boss says he'd like to get them all together in something like Gilmore Stadium, fine them, or anything. Maybe a three month build up. Just to get them out where they could see each other! Feel their strength, solidarity. Hell, they don't know what they belong to!" (from an interview with a staff member in a large local).

Those leadership groups which must hold the consent of their members will probably eventually use the method of fining those who do not attend in order to "get people out." Though it goes against the conviction of many leaders, it has the demonstrable effect of bringing the members out and subjecting them to union experience.

Mexican and Negro Attendance at General Membership Meetings:

The General Membership meeting has a usual ten per cent or less of the local's members in attendance, yet it is here that the ordinary member has the most access to the structure of the local. Mexican and Negro members, in view of their general position in the society, might be expected to take advantage of this access in atypical fashion. The data do not indicate they do so in any very consistent fashion. Their attendance varies, generally, with that of the membership as a whole. However, when an index of attendance is computed by taking the proportion of the ethnic group attending as a fraction of that of the entire membership, important differences among Mexican and Negro ethnic contigents appear.

If the very small ethnic contingents (sixty members or less) are omitted from the sample, there remain thirteen substantial Negro populations and fifteen Mexican populations. Separating these into locals where the ethnic group is (1) highly over-represented at these meetings (2) represented at an average rate and (3) under-represented, there are five Negro contingents heavily over-represented, eight with average attendance, <u>none</u> with extremely low attendance. Mexicans, in contrast, are over-represented in only two locals and average in six. They are under-represented in all of the seven remaining locals.

The very small contingents of Mexicans or Negroes are omitted because they have a consistently low rate of attendance; the average for these five contingents is about one-fourth of that for the entire memberships involved. It is likely that in locals where there is no organization of an ethnic bloc by professional leaders the small groups of these workers will participate in a very half-hearted way. They are marginal, both to the labor force and to the union organization (and, very likely, because of exclusionist hiring practices).

Where the ethnic population is large, participation in General Membership meetings is related to specifically ethnic organization. In the five locals where Negro attendance is far above the norm, this is a result of organization on ethnic lines by either left wing or race leadership. This high participation is accompanied by Negro access to leadership positions; in all but one of these locals they are represented on the executive board, and in that one their high participation is alleged to be one reason for "throwing the local into receivership." In the two locals where Mexican participation is remarkably high there is likewise evidence of race participation. In one local Mexican political factions are dominant; in the other, left wing leaders sponsor both Mexican and Negro participation, and both minorities are represented on the executive board.

In considering the lower rate of participation by Mexicans, it is important to remember that they ordinarily constitute a larger proportion of the total members than do Negroes; they may participate at an average rate or lower and still dominate the General Membership meetings in many locals. Though their attendance is not above average, they are from one-third to one half of those present at the usual General Membership meetings in four locals. Thus it can be said that Mexicans have the advantage of numbers and Negroes that of more intensive participation in General Membership meetings.

Mexicans and Negroes: Cultural Barriers vs. Social:

In interpreting this difference in participation, the general position of the two ethnic populations in the larger society is important. Mexican-Americans, with a bi-cultural background, may have difficulties with language and the culture generally which tend to reduce participation in voluntary organizations and thus in the locals (9). Such an explanation occurred frequently in discussions with union leaders, especially those responsible for the organizing of workers who know little about the union from personal experience.

One organizer in a low status, low wage industry, put it this way.

> "Their reaction is either noncommittal or very hostile-- 'I don't have no use for the god damn union.' But the big majority will listen to you and say nothing. You don't know where you are with them. Then, if their

> leaders say join, they'll join--but with all kinds of mental reservations."

This organizer saw a resistance due to both the alien nature of the union idea, and the presence of anti-union values in the Mexican-American culture, due both to their Spanish-American heritage and their position in the American society.

> "How many times have I heard this, when I called at people's houses--'Why don't you get the foreman to tell us to join; then we'll join!' I think the old padrone system, which existed in Mexico, is part of the reason. The Mexican has a sort of loyalty to the boss; he always thinks the boss is morally right. Jimmy here (another organizer), calls it 'militant servility' and by God he's pretty close to it."

Another factor, however, is the greater permeability of job and status barriers (in unionized work at least) to mobile Mexicans. This is clearly indicated in the data on relative occupational levels of Mexicans and Negroes in this sample. If "ethnic self consciousness" is seen as a response to barriers based on ethnic criteria, then the relative weakness of such barriers for Mexicans should lower Mexican ethnic identification. At the same time, there would be fewer objective reasons for organizing on an ethnic basis.

Mexican workers range from Spanish speaking illiterates to American-born high school graduates with skilled or white-collar jobs. One end of this continuum is likely to be isolated from the union culture complex while the other end will have a lesser need for the specifically ethnic forms of organization and perhaps a lesser need for the union as an instrument of job protection and mobility. In such an interpretation, union participation is easier, objectively, for those Mexican-Americans who have the least need of it.

For Negroes, however, there is little opportunity available to assimilate, "pass," or move upward in the limited status hierarchy of warehouse, factory and store. Since they are more and more likely to be educated through secondary school and since their job ceiling is lower than that for Mexicans, a greater disparity between abilities and opportunities is to be expected. From this one can expect a greater militancy aimed at the barriers and, at the same time, a higher incidence of leadership abilities among those most injured. Such a probability is confirmed by statements of many leaders whose locals include large Negro contingents. The Business Agent of one laborers' local remarked:

"The Negroes are brighter and are better members of the local. And that's one of the troubles, though I wouldn't tell any of the members. The Negro members are much higher grade men than most of the whites. That causes trouble. In the last election they elected eight Negroes and four whites. (The membership is divided fifty-fifty.) The white guys bitched about it, but the hell of it was, they wouldn't nominate!
I know the executive board felt pretty discouraged about it. Well then, two vacancies came up and I appointed white guys to balance the board. I think that'll make it easier."

In short, the same jobs which select the pick of the Negro work force (since they provide at least security on the job) are likely to select the marginal members of the "white" work force. This is probably less often true of Mexican-American workers.

Thus the factors producing a low rate of Mexican participation can be read in reverse for Negro members. Their higher rates of participation (especially ethnic participation) reflects (1) the more uniform and intimidating barriers to mobility (2) a greater ethnic self-consciousness, resulting from both objective difficulties in mobility and the nature of their ethnic status and (3) a cultural background which makes communication of the "union idea" easier to Negroes than to Mexicans.

Attendance at Special Election Meetings:

The attendance of members at the Special Election meetings is much higher and more uniform than at the General Membership meetings. This is to be expected, since these meetings concern the vital interests of the members-- contract conditions, dues structure, strike action and the election of union officers. As labor leaders put it, "When the chips are down the boys will come out," and this level of participation is the one most emphasized when the democratic nature of the unions is discussed.

The range is from one-third to two-thirds of the members attending, or proportions comparable to the general population's voting in national elections. The median per cent in attendance for the twelve locals where data are available is forty-six per cent, with half the locals between thirty-five and fifty-five per cent. Mexicans and Negroes attend these meetings at about the same rate as the general membership if all locals are aggregated; the median per cent attending for ethnic contingents and for the non-ethnic members is within five per cent of the average for the whole. However, there is some inconsistency from local to local.

If the contingents of ethnic members are divided into those sharply above average, average, and below average, seven locals have a high proportion of one or the other population (Mexicans, Negroes, or others) attending election meetings. In these same locals, the relative attendance of this over-represented population is also high at the General Membership meetings, while the increase in attendance at election meetings is substantially higher than that for either of the remaining populations. These cases give evidence of ethnic over-participation at a crucial point in the control system of the local; at these meetings important policy decisions are made, if such decisions are at all subject to membership consent.

In all of these locals with ethnic organization among the members, the over-represented population has an average job level at least equal to that of the members as a whole. Ethnic power is most prevalent where it is least needed. Such ethnic-tinged participation is not, usually, the result of explicit organization; despite its continuity through time, the basis may be obscured. In the words of one local leader: "Negroes and white guys are on opposite sides of the fence on every issue except-- and this is funny-- anything having to do with race."

Extremely high participation in a local's election meetings does not necessarily mean a given contingent will dominate those meetings. Electoral dominance is based on both rate of participation and number, and the most important factor in accounting for ethnic dominance in these locals is, simply, proportion of the total membership. This is illustrated by the following table.

TABLE 3-1

NEGRO AND MEXICAN CONTINGENTS AS PROPORTIONS OF* MEMBERSHIP AND OF SPECIAL ELECTION MEETINGS

PROPORTION OF MEMBERSHIP	Proportion of Special Election Meetings .00-.14	.15-.29	.30-.44	.45-.59	.60-.75
.00-.14	6				
.15-.29	1	5	1		
.30-.44	1	1	1	1	1
.45-.59			1	1	2
.60-.75					1

* Omitted are locals which have fined meetings and those in which a given ethnic contingent is made up of sixty or fewer members.

Although a large proportion of the total membership is usually necessary to dominate the meetings, the over-represented contingents are majorities of those present in five locals. And, dominant or not, the highly represented population is always a substantial part of those attending Special Election meetings.

Mexican and Negro attendance at these meetings is proportional to their total membership and not to their hold on the better jobs; in fact, both groups are consistently over-represented in this respect. The ethnic members in low-level jobs, who avoid the routine meetings, evidently turn out in proportional numbers at the key meetings, as do union members in general.

THE LEADERS OF THE LOCALS

Attendance at meetings has been used as a rough index of participation in the local union: the assumption is made that an investment of time and energy in the organized structure of the union reflects the importance of the union to the member. The study of participation is, then, a study of the function of the union from the member's point of view. It is, at the same time, a study of the conditions within which the formal structure and its leaders must function.

The leaders of the local union may also be studied as expressions of the ordinary member's share of the union, for they may be defined as <u>representatives</u> of the membership. In this frame-of-reference, the degree to which significant strata of the membership are represented in the formal hierarchy is an important question. Two kinds of strata are particularly important in this respect: one is ethnic identification and the other, closely related, is skill level.

Types of Leadership Position:

Local union leaders may be conveniently divided into three classes: (1) the plantwide rank and file leaders (stewards and grievance committeemen), (2) the "localwide" rank and file leaders (unpaid officers and executive board members) and (3) the professional, full-time leaders (business agents, secretary-treasurers, and sometimes, international representatives).

The plantwide officers are the channels of communication between union hall and workplace. They are the most immediate and continuous ties the members have with the total union organization. By far the most common class of union leaders, their formal power is restricted but they are in a position where advancement into the "localwide" leadership is possible. (While all plantwide leaders do not become "localwide" leaders, most "localwide" leaders start at the plant level.)

The "localwide" leaders' orientation is to the entire local

organization. Constituting the local's Executive Board, they are consulted in the first formal stages of the decision-making process, and their vote may be final. They are also supposed to serve as "watchdogs for the rank and file," vis a vis the paid staff.

Professional leaders fall into two classes, according to their position in relation to the controlling force of the local. A leader is either chosen by that force (the membership's vote or the international's hierarchy) or else appointed by someone who is. To be precise, the former type is the true union leader, with formal power and responsibility for making important decisions. Appointed officers have a lower status job (" I'm just a hired hand around here," as one remarked) and less power, but their influence is sufficiently important to justify including them in the professional leadership staff of the locals.

Professional leaders are usually better paid than the highest paid members and they spend all of their time working for the local. Their jobs include "policing the contract" through circulating among the shops and contacting stewards, management and members; collecting dues if there is no check-off and supervising check-offs if there are any: negotiating contracts and preparing cases for arbitration, then attempting to influence arbitration: keeping in touch with other significant organizations (other unions in the locality and other levels of the international) ; attending and helping to "run" the executive board's meetings and the General Membership meetings in the local and organizing new members. While there is usually some job specialization among the staff members of a local, if the staff is small each may be responsible for all of these matters.

It is possible to have considerable confidence in the data for the representation of ethnic members in the leadership structure of the locals. The number of individuals involved is relatively small and easy for the informants to remember, while professional leaders are particularly sensitive to individuals in positions of formal responsibility. Reliability is highest with regard to professional staff and executive board members, lower in the case of stewards. The local leaders interviewed gave, in every case, the name and job level of the executive board's current members, as well as their ethnic identity. Thus the data on board members and staff is not only a most useful index of ethnic participation, it is also a reliable one. While the information on stewards is not as accurate, it is roughly so, as the stewards usually have functional importance for the leader and most locals have periodic meetings of their stewards when the group is visible as a whole.

The Representation of Mexicans and Negroes in Leadership Positions:

The 63,000 union members in this sample are represented by approximately 1,300 officers, ranging from chief stewards to managers of the locals. Eight hundred and forty-five are stewards, almost 400 are executive board members, and seventy-nine are professional staff members. Negro and Mexican members together are forty per cent of the total membership in these locals. They are fifty-six per cent of the chief stewards, thirty-one per cent of the executive board members, and twenty-eight per cent of the staff members. (The ethnic identity of these officers in four kinds of unions is given in Table IV, Appendix "A").

Mexicans and Negroes are, thus, over-represented at only one level, that of steward. This high level of representation does not occur consistently, however. Instead, it is found chiefly among the craft-type locals and, since the craftsmans and customer service workers locals have a low steward rate, the chief reason for the over representation is predominance as stewards in the one-job laborers' locals. They are represented at above average rate in these locals and are proportionally represented in the industrial locals as stewards.

In order to show variation from local to local, an index of representation is derived by taking the proportion of officers from a given ethnic contingent as a fraction of the proportion of total membership from that contingent. Since the measure results in extreme values when the denominator is very small, those ethnic populations constituting less than ten per cent of the total members are omitted. The results are presented in summary form below.

TABLE 3-2
AVERAGE INDEXES OF REPRESENTATION FOR MEXICANS AND NEGROES IN LEADERSHIP POSITIONS

LEADERSHIP POSITION	Number of Locals	Average Index	Range of Indexes	Locals with None
Staff*				
Mexicans	10	.42	.00-1.34	4
Negroes	8	.38	.00-1.13	5
Executive Board				
Mexicans	17	.65	.00-2.08	1
Negroes	14	.59	.00-1.83	4
Stewards**				
Mexicans	16	.92	.22-2.00	0
Negroes	14	.82	.00-1.65	1

* Staff index not computed for one man staffs.

** Locals without steward system omitted.

The range of representation is very wide, as inspection of the detailed data for each local shows (Table V, Appendix "A"). The percentage of Mexican stewards varies with the proportion of the membership Mexican, though usually below it; the percentage of Negro stewards varies in a less consistent way and is, on the average, somewhat lower proportionally. Complete lack of representation is rare for either group at the steward level.

Executive board membership, limited by a possible number of positions only about one-half that of the stewards, exhibits more fluctuation. The average indexes are below proportional representational, centering about sixty per cent of what would be expected if Mexicans and Negroes were represented according to their numbers in the membership. Variation is greater here and five ethnic contingents are unrepresented in locals where they are ten per cent or more of the total members.

The index of representation at staff level is still lower for both Mexicans and Negroes, averaging around forty per cent of proportional representation. One-half of the contingents for which indexes were computed have no representation at staff level.

Representation of the "Residual Members" in Leadership Positions:

While there is a certain amount of difference between the representation of these two ethnic minorities in the locals, with one or the other over-represented at certain levels in certain locals, the residual membership, or those members who are neither Mexican or Negro, is consistently over-represented at every level. This reflects, not the relative size of this population, but its share of leadership positions in proportion to its size in the membership. In only a very few cases are both Mexicans and Negroes over-represented. Residual members are under-represented as stewards in only five locals (and sharply under-represented in only three), as executive board members in three locals, and as staff members in only one local with a staff including two or more members.

The over-representation of the non-Negro/Mexican members is indicated in the table on page 57.

The decline in over-representation of residual members from AFL industrial locals to CIO locals is particularly noticeable. Over-representation is substantial for all categories of locals and offices except for stewards in the CIO unions. This rank

TABLE 3-3
OVER-REPRESENTATION OF RESIDUAL POPULATIONS
IN FOUR TYPES OF LOCAL UNION

TYPE OF LOCAL	STEWARDS $\overline{M}$ Index	Rank	EXEC. BD $\overline{M}$ Index	Rank	STAFF* $\overline{M}$ Index	Rank
AFL Industrial	1.87	1	1.83	1	2.44	1
One-job Laborer	1.48	2	1.40	3	1.78	2
Cust. S. & Craft.	1.11	3	1.49	2	1.61	3
CIO Industrial	1.01	4	1.33	4	1.38	4

* In computing the index for staff, omitting locals noted in Table 3-2, twelve locals were used; four AFL Industrial, two one-job laborer, three customer service and craftsmans and four CIO locals.

order in reverse indicates clearly those locals in which Negroes and Mexicans most nearly approximate proportional representation in the leadership, while the rank order of leadership positions, from steward to staff members, indicates those offices in which they are most apt to be represented. Representation declines as the importance of the office increases and, as representation declines, the variation among locals increases.

PARTICIPATION AND REPRESENTATION

Attendance and Representation:

Attendance of ethnic members at the meetings of the locals should, theoretically, affect representation in the control structure of the local. Those ethnic contingents who attend the Special Election meetings should be proportionally represented in the leadership structure. In testing this proposition, the proportion of board members from a given ethnic population is taken as a fraction of the ethnic group's proportion of Special Election meetings. The average indexes are not, in fact, very different from those based simply on the ethnic proportion of the local's membership. Ethnic members do not appear on executive boards in proportion to their attendance at Special Election meetings.

This may indicate a lack of interest in putting "their own

men'' into office, but it is more likely a result of weakness in the leadership of Mexican and Negro contingents. It is significant that the three locals in which Mexicans or Negroes are over-represented on the basis of attendance at Special Election meetings all have powerful ethnic factions in the membership. Well organized ethnic contingents will be represented on the executive board of their local, but unorganized populations are much less likely to make their votes count no matter how large they may be.

Interrelations Between Representation at Different Levels:

The average representation for both Mexicans and Negroes at professional staff level is less than half of what would be proportional to their part of the membership. When the Mexican and Negro proportion of the staff is based on their proportion of the executive boards in the same locals, however, a close relationship is indicated. Taking the ethnic proportion of the staff as a fraction of the ethnic proportion of the executive board for each local, the average ratio for Mexicans is 1.00 and that for Negroes, 1.08. Although these ratios range from zero to over 2.00 in various locals, there were only two cases of the nineteen analyzed in which the ethnic population was represented on the executive board and not on the staff; there were no cases where Mexicans or Negroes were in a staff position but had no representation on the board. Such an association indicates that ethnic representation on the executive board of a local represents real power. There were, however, a number of locals in which large Mexican or Negro contingents had no representation on the board (See Table 3-2 above.)

The steward position is the one leadership level at which ethnic contingents have more than their proportional representation. Participation in steward roles is not, however, consistently related to representation on the executive board of the locals. Of the larger Mexican or Negro contingents (one-tenth of the total members or more) in locals with steward systems, thirty-seven in all, only three are unrepresented as stewards. However, of the thirty-four represented in the steward position, only twenty-five are also represented on the executive board; nine are not. This indicates a loose relation between representation at the two levels of leadership. There are locals with very few stewards from a given ethnic contingent, who nevertheless have heavy executive board weighting from that group, and locals with a substantial proportion of ethnic stewards and no executive board representatives from the same ethnic group.

Nor is there a close relationship between the presence of stewards and staff members from the same ethnic minority; of those which have representation at steward position, only one-third are represented at the staff level. Thus there is little evidence that participation of ethnic union members as stewards means much where power and prestige in the locals are concerned. If this is the lowest rung in the leadership ladder, that ladder is frequently a one-rung affair. The appointment of Mexicans and Negroes to steward positions seems frequently to be a device for cooptation, the placation of a dissident or restless minority.

THE RECRUITMENT PATTERNS OF ETHNIC LEADERS

Leadership mobility in the locals flows through certain channels, and from these the possibilities of ethnic leadership mobility may be inferred. The first step in movement upward within the industrial locals is movement in the job hierarchy. Stewards come from the more highly skilled ranks of the industrial union's membership and in locals where Mexicans or Negroes dominate the skilled job categories they also dominate the steward corps.

From steward the "active" usually moves to office in the "localwide" organization, either as a member-at-large of the executive board or as an officer. In this position he is able to develope influence and familiarity with the members and personal relations with the professional staff. His move into the staff will be either through election (in which case he is frequently sponsored by the professional leaders) or through appointment by the top leader. As an elected or appointed local officer he is then known to the international hierarchy and may be "taken up" into the rank of international representative or, occasionally, international vice-president.

As illustrations of ethnic mobility, two brief career histories are presented.

The Case of Juan:

Juan Garcia went to work as a young man in a middle-sized refractory in the southern part of Los Angeles County. There were many Mexicans working there, for this low paying and strenuous work did not attract the more advantaged members of the work force.

"You see, they'd come in, maybe jump the fence at San Diego and get jobs working at very low wages. Then the employer would keep 'em quiet anytime they griped; he could always say, "Suppose I tell the Immigration about you, then where'd you be?" That way the employer could get a lot of extra work out of you. And the Mexicans, they didn't speak very well and didn't know too much about their rights anyway, and they made good workers for the boss."

Juan had advantages that the pioneer Mexicans in this labor force had lacked. He had finished high school, spoke good English, and could think more "along American lines" as he put it. He quickly reached the job of pressman and made good wages.

"Now before the war I was already working in the union there. I was chief steward. Then in the early days of the war this thing happened..." Juan lead a walk-out because the company would not pay the "going rate." The plant was doing war work, however, and both a "Navy Brass and an Army Captain" came in. Juan explained the strike as the fault of the "Boss." " 'We didn't shut it down I tell you,' I said, 'There's the guy' and I pointed at the Manager.' Well, he gave us the raise and the plant was back on schedule; we went right out rounding up the night shift."

"You know, twenty-one days later I was in Camp Roberts, totin' a gun!"

When Juan came back after three years in the European theatre, the union was "pretty well shot-- three foremen were shop stewards!" Juan then organized a coalition of Okies, Negroes and Mexicans, persuaded the three "stewards" to resign and ran for chief steward. At the same time he helped sign up every worker in the plant.

He was recently hired as a regional organizer and business agent. "One reason the union has me now as BA is they got to deal with the Mexicans-- we're almost a majority. The big thing is, the main problem is, showing them <u>how</u> the union works and where it will benefit them."

"Me, I left the highest paid job in the Refractory for this. The pay just don't compare. But, you meet interesting people and..." Juan did not finish, but he told some stories.

"When I was in Houston, Texas, in uniform during the war, me and two other fellers go into a joint and get some coffee and pie. When we go to pay the guy says 'That'll be fifteen and fifteen' and to me he says, 'That'll be twenty-five.' 'What the Hell,' I say, 'Look, this guy's a corporal and this one's a sergeant and I'm just a private.' Well, he looks at me and says 'They're <u>white</u>.'

"...Well, this kid my cousin confessed he stole the generator off the car. I didn't see how, or what they did with it. He told me though, when they got to the station the cops beat the hell out of them. 'We was ready to tell them anything after they beat us up long enough.' "

When visiting relatives in Arizona, Juan was urged to leave his son there, so he wouldn't grow up to become a "pachuco." " 'No sir,' I told her, 'This boy's coming back to Los Angeles with me, where he can act like anybody else. Not a Mexican.'

Well, my boy has done all right; no "pachuco" stuff for him. He's working in the lab at the refractory now, good job, and working at commercial art at night. The firm offered to send him to U.S.C. to study ceramics, but he'd rather go on with his art."

"We need organization. The only way we can get any improvement for the Negroes and Mexicans and Orientals is work at it ourselves. And that's one reason for me being in this union."

The Case of Johnny:

Johnny Watson came to Los Angeles during the 1930's, "when things were pretty tough." After a number of jobs, he got a decent shift at the Los Angeles Transit Company, maintaining street-cars. It was not bad, for a Negro.

However, there was no future in it. It was particularly hard on a person to watch new workers go right into the well paid jobs while older hands remained as sweepers and "heavy mechanics."

When the war boom began jobs opened up in shipyards and aircraft factories but Negroes weren't being hired. Still, jobs were vacated by some of those who were hired. Johnny, pressed by mounting costs of living, quit the Los Angeles Transit Company and went to work at a foundry. The work was hot and hard but there was opportunity to go up. White workers were deserting the heavy work in droves, leaving big holes in the job pyramid.

Johnny was promoted to helper and then to molder-- he was the first Negro in Los Angeles to hold such a high ranking job. He became even more active in the local, and it was a union which appreciated the activity of a Negro. He was appointed as an organizer, full time, and was later elected by a referendum of the members who were more and more likely to be Negroes or Mexicans.

His work is hard and sometimes depressing. Negroes are only in the heaviest industry, where they are less than five per cent semiskilled and, for the rest, "They get the jobs that require a strong back and a weak brain."

"There's less discrimination against Negro union guys than white guys by the foreman; you see, they figure a minority guy that reaches a union position still feels he's inferior and so he won't be militant. Management looks to Negroes and Mexicans to go ahead on a speed-up practice; they figure after they do the rest will follow. The minute a Negro resists the speedup, he's fodder for being shot at. They will use every means to get you-- absenteeism, tardiness, unauthorized leave-- anything you do."

"People are sure funny though. I'm taking an art class downtown and there's a guy there that's working away at painting besides me. He's friendly. But one night we got to talking about race and you know he made my blood run cold. He was a regular Ku Kluxer! Not with me, of course; just with Negroes in general."

Johnny's job is organizing and it is a hard job to do, for his local is one known as "left wing" and is out of the CIO, with little organizational support. Organizing in steel is hard enough anyway, "Nobody has organized over fifteen per cent-- the Steelworkers don't do anything either and its sure tough enough. Locally you have to take into account the Merchant's and Manufacturers' Association, where these little bucket shops get all kinds of support."

"The Negro guys are mostly from the South and those from the South just sit back and wait. They gotta be shown. I don't think there's any difference in organizing by race, if the <u>region</u> is the same, though."

The Craft-Local Dichotomy and Ethnic Representation:

Mexican and Negro professional staff members in the sample are a small population but one of the greatest importance; it is likely that in every case their mobility was due to ethnic issues and ethnic participation. The case histories of Johnny and Juan indicate the way such officers move upwards in the industrial unions. In the craft type locals the pattern is different. The lack of job differentiation gives all workers an even break and, since Mexicans and Negroes are heavily concentrated in some of these locals, they reach the leadership level by organizing influence or gaining admittance to the inner circles of the administration.

In fact there is, ironically, a better chance that Negro and Mexican workers will be represented in the craft-type unions than in the industrial locals. Thus, of the one-job laborers' membership, fifty-seven per cent are Mexicans or Negroes and in these unions of janitors, dishwashers and building construction laborers sixty per cent of the executive board members are also Negro or Mexican. However, in the industrial locals one-third of the Negroes and Mexicans are unskilled and they amount to over fifteen per cent of the total membership-- but in these locals the unskilled workers are almost unrepresented. The heavy preponderance of skilled workers on the executive boards is evident in the following table.

TABLE 3-4
COMPOSITION OF EXECUTIVE BOARDS BY SKILL LEVELS: INDUSTRIAL LOCALS

COMPOSITION OF BOARD	NO. LOCALS	JOB LEVEL SK.	S-SK.	U-SK.	TOTAL MEMBERS
Skilled Members Only	5	83			83
Skilled & S-Sk. but no U-Sk.	3	38	48		86
Skilled & S-Sk. and U-Sk.	3	34	31	11	76
	11*	155	79	11	245
Proportion		.63	.32	.04	.99

*Data incomplete for Textile Workers and Shipyard Workers Locals.

Of 245 executive board members only four per cent are unskilled laborers. Even if all of these were Negro or Mexican the unskilled workers from these contingents would be represented at about one-third of proportional representation.

The same organizational barriers which, in craft-organized work, make it easier for Mexicans or Negroes to be segregated in the low pay, low status jobs, makes it easier for them to gain representation in the political system of the local, for they are usually a dominant bloc of voters in these one-job laborers' locals. The freedom which allows them to move to higher jobs in the industrial unions, since it throws them into a voting constituency in which they are quantitative minorities, gives the unskilled ethnic worker little chance for office.

The skill bias is as strong as the ethnic bias in the selection of leaders. Skilled workers are thirty-eight per cent of the members in the locals, but their representation index is 1.65; semiskilled workers, forty per cent, have an index of .80: the unskilled, twenty-two per cent of the members, have an overall rate of .23. Skill differences are, if anything, more important than ethnic differences. This is less striking, however, when it is remembered that over two-thirds of the unskilled labor force in these locals is Mexican or Negro. The bias against unskilled workers and that against ethnic workers in leadership positions are nearly identical.

Situation of the Ethnic Leader:

In both types of local, craft and industrial, Mexican and Negro professional leaders usually arise only when there is a very large proportion of ethnic members. With the exception of one local which pro-rates ethnic staff members, no local in the sample with less than forty per cent ethnic membership has either Mexican or Negro staff members. The average ethnic fraction in these locals is sixty per cent. Further, there is usually a large number of members of the leader's own ethnic identity, averaging one-third of the membership for both Mexican and Negro leaders.

Most of the locals with a Mexican or Negro professional leader have only one such leader on their staff. (three-fourths of the cases). This isolation of ethnic leaders is due in part to the small number of staff positions available, but it also reflects the "minority group representative" character of such positions. All Mexican and Negro leaders are, among other things, race leaders. They speak for their fellows in the councils of the local and they carry these councils back to the ethnic members.

In two locals having only one staff member, he is Mexican; there is no case of a Negro as the sole professional leader of a union. Except for the Packinghouse Workers, of the CIO (where the Negro is regional director) there are no cases of Negro members on any local staff with less than four members. The average size of the staffs having Negro members is eight, that of those with Mexican members, five. Thus the Negro professional leader is apt to be the only Negro on a large local's staff; the Mexican may be the only staff member or one of a small number of professional leaders. This indicates that the Negro union leader is most likely to be primarily a race specialist while the Mexican leader may take the more generalized role of the union leader.

SUMMARY: PARTICIPATION AND LEADERSHIP

The entry of ethnic minorities into the organizational structure of labor unions may be seen as a three step process. First and most crucial is the entry of the ethnic contingent to the labor force of the industry. Second is their entry into the union, not only as card-carriers and dues payers, but as active participants in organizational meetings. Finally there is the movement of Mexicans or Negroes into the leadership hierarchy of the local, culminating in elevation to the International Union's hierarchy.

Once they have entered an industrial work force, Mexicans seem to be somewhat more difficult and Negroes easier to organize than are the non-ethnic workers. If the union has a union-shop clause in its contract, however, as do the majority of these locals, this is not important. A sharper diagnostic tool is the study of attendance at organizational meetings, which distinguishes between the "paper" membership and the participating membership. Three kinds of meetings were studied; the results may be summarized as follows.

A. Mexicans and Negroes participate in Plant Unit meetings in proportion to their length of time in the labor force and job level.

B. In General Membership meetings Negroes participate at a higher rate than average, Mexicans at a consistently lower than average rate.

C. In special Election meetings both Negroes and Mexicans participate at the average rate or higher. Certain locals are marked by extreme over-participation of one ethnic contingent and correspondingly low rates for the others.

D. The quantitative domination of a meeting does not follow from a very high rate of attendance by an ethnic group, but when such attendance does occur that group will be well represented as a fraction of those in attendance.

Attendance rates for the ethnic groups are associated with their relative job-levels, but for Mexicans attendance is lower and Negroes higher than would be expected on the basis of their proportion of skilled and semi-skilled jobs. Mexicans generally have a higher job-level than do Negroes, reflecting their earlier entry into the work forces and their greater numbers, but Negro members' attendance rates are usually higher at any skill level.

The proportion of Special Election meetings made up of an ethnic group is no better means of predicting their share in the leadership positions than is their proportion in the membership of the local. Both Mexicans and Negroes are represented at the average rate or higher as stewards, at slightly above one-half proportional on the executive boards and at some forty per cent of proportional on the professional staffs of the locals.

There is a relationship between skill-level and stewardship; in those locals with large proportions of the skilled workers Negro or Mexican , these populations have substantial representation as stewards. This does not carry over in any consistent fashion to the next highest level of leadership, however; though large contingents are apt to have representation on the executive board, the amount of representation is not clearly related to proportion of members, proportion of stewards, or proportion of skilled workers. There is thus a shaky rung in the leadership ladder between the position of steward and that of executive board member.

Mexicans and Negro contingents represented on the executive boards are, however, much more apt to have staff representation than those unrepresented. Though the rates vary greatly, most locals with ethnic board members have ethnic staff members and no local has staff representation without executive board representation from the same ethnic contingent.

The probability of a Mexican or Negro member's arriving at a staff position in the industrial locals may be roughly calculated in this fashion: (1) his chances of entering the labor force (2) multiplied by his chances of reaching a skilled job (3) multiplied by his chances of reaching a steward position, (4) his chances of reaching "localwide" office and (5) his chances of election or appointment to the Staff.

The rungs of the ladder are fewer but further apart in the usual craft-type local. The steps are simply (1) entry to the work force (2) appointment as steward (rare except in one-job locals) (3) appointment or election to the board and (4) the staff. The officer corps is much smaller in these locals and only in the one-job unions does the ethnic individual have much chance.

Ironically, his chances are better in one-job locals than in industrial locals, since he is apt to have an unskilled job in either case and since unskilled Mexicans and Negroes are much more highly represented as leaders in one-job locals than in the industrial locals of the sample. Executive boards of industrial locals are heavily biased towards a membership made up of "skilled mechanics."

Those Mexicans and Negroes who reach the top of the ladder in the local union organization are usually isolated from others of their own ethnic identity. In the cases of Negro leaders particularly, each is apt to be the only Negro among eight or more other staff members. The job is heavily laden with ethnic implications. "They represent the minority guys."

CHAPTER IV

ROLE OF THE LOCAL UNION LEADER: DETERMINANTS AND DILEMMAS

Participation in the local union and representation in the leadership are only the surface phenomena of union politics. While it is important to know the relative attendance of ethnic minorities at the formal meetings of the unions and their share in the formal leadership offices, these data do not allow one to estimate the utility of the local union as an instrument to represent the interests of ethnic members.

An analysis of the control structure of the local union is necessary, in order to relate participation and representation to the action of the union as an ongoing, organized group. The recruitment of the ethnic labor leader has been described; it is now necessary to analyze the role system into which he moves. In doing so, the focus of inquiry shifts from union activity as an effect variable, to the union structure as an explanatory variable. "Representation" becomes control; "participation" becomes activation of the members. The unit of analysis is no longer a category of persons related only by "common fate"--it is the formal and informal organization of the local union, the role system moving through time.

The professional leader has a preponderant weight in the day to day policy making of the local; his role is a key unit for the analysis of the union power structure and, hence, of policy formation on ethnic issues. From the point of view of the professional leader, the power-structure of the local is revealed as a working process, forcing decision and defining alternatives. At the same time, more than the leader's role is illuminated, for his role is an organic part of the union as a social group, and in studying it one moves towards the roots of the union structure.

CONFLICTS AND ACCOMODATIONS

In this analysis, the functions of the union movement will be considered as independent variables, dictating the kind of concrete goals which union leaders must achieve. If the goals are "wages, hours and working conditions," they will limit the kinds of organization which will survive; the organization will, in turn, select individuals who will "work" and they, from their point of view, will try to "keep their jobs in the union movement" (14).

Unions constitute an organizational complex which serves to structure certain unstable and crucial relationships in the evolving culture of industrial work. The most general statement of the problem to be solved is the resolution of conflict between what the workers expect and the dynamic, autocratic nature of the work situation. As one solution, the American union movement has been a protest movement from its origins-- one which evolved a roughly standardized set of norms and techniques, including a role-system and its accompanying self definitions. This standardized culture complex then spread to other areas where the original precipitating factors were active, or, as union organizers say, "When the situation looks ripe in a plant, we move in." Once in, the union redefines the work situation, establishing what Slichter has called an "industrial jurisprudence," or a common law of work (36). This law, backed by the punitive force of the union, serves to regulate conflicts in the areas of management-worker relations-- those centered about tenure of the job, authority relations with management and, perhaps most important, relative share of the industrial income, or wages.

However, as noted in previous discussions, a wide variation is seen in the type of local unions which can serve these functions. This means that the local leader's role varies widely-- in the nature of the job, the degree of security and the power that it confers. These aspects will be considered in detail later; first it is important to note those elements of the leadership situation common to all union leaders. Two stand out clearly; one is the conflict between protest and accomodation, the other, the conflict between administrative roles and the democratic dogma.

Sacred Ideology and Secular Compromise:

The basic strength of all unions lies in their ability to organize the workers against a management that seeks to identify its interests with the conservative values of the culture. The union is always, in this primitive sense, a protest organization. All union leaders are at times in the position of arousing the members "against the Boss" and the boss's ideology-- until an agreement has been made and the necessity of living with management supercedes protest and forces accomodation. The protest motif must be kept alive but it must also be controlled.

Certain analogues come to mind, of which Myrdal's portrait of the accomodative race leader is most striking (27). In the unions, as among Negroes in the South, one sees a group of leaders organizing the protest of individually helpless members in order to affect power relations. The process is one of continual bargaining, for the protest organized is dependent upon the carrying structure (white society or corporate management) and moves through compromise after compromise. Yet the mobilization of the followers depends upon using a sacred ideology, stressing the absolute values of "equality, our people, the workers."

And in the unions as in the race organization one finds a differential association between leaders of the depressed group (as against members) and the leaders of the powerful group. Given the necessities of bargaining, there is the concomitant responsibility on the part of the accomodative leader to a compromise solution. Wildcat strikes are controlled and their leaders punished; the contract in general is honored. Still, in the final analysis, the power of the leader depends upon his ability to lead the members <u>against</u> the company. These members have a different frame of reference for understanding relations with the company and frequently they cannot be convinced on what are, for the leader, rational grounds. The upshot is, frequently, ideology, the solution of a real conflict in interests by the application of verbal medicine (25).

Charismatic Leader and Bureaucratic Administrator:

At the same time the leader faces a conflict between his personal position as an administrator and democratic processes as they usually work out. His status is higher than that of his highest ranking members, and the discrepancy increases as the job level of the members is lower. His job is always organizational and administrative, whether his members are photoengravers or janitors. His work is highly specialized and requires a wide range of uncommon skills, yet his tenure in office is at the mercy of elections. These, in turn, are at the mercy of a membership which does not fully understand his work, the union's situation or the resulting committments. Thus the conflict arises between his democratic function as spokesman for the members on one hand and his job as an administrator and a technical specialist on the other. The two functions may collide head-on.

An "old fashioned" leader for one craft local put it this way:

> "Well, I'll tell you, its pitiful. Your members don't know what's going on anymore. You have to be a labor lawyer and an economist and a labor relations expert to get by now. In the old days you never wrote a contract. You made a bargain by word of mouth and shook hands on it. You went back to the members and said (spreading his arms wide) 'Boys, here it is!' And that was it.

> "You find nowadays that a guy comes to you and says 'You agreed to such and so.' And you said 'Did I?' and he pulls out the contract and finds it. We have to have our contracts all approved by the International now; we have to get the bugs out of it.
> "Our members are more or less helpless about a lot of things. I tell you it's sad; they aren't lawyers and they've got the union and all at heart-- but you've got to know too much nowadays."

From this perspective, the tendency for locals to be controlled by machines and informal deals is understandable; there is a limit to the instability that can be built into a given organizational position if that position requires personnel of definite abilities. At the same time the leader, as he values his status and as his tenure depends upon the accomodation of conflicting pressures at the roots of the union's strength, will tend to give a high value to any stabilization of those pressures.

The powers with which he treats for the benefit of his members are in some cases easier to come to a permanent understanding with than are the members. The result is that some leadership groups identify with management, just as some Negro leaders identify with whites and are in a position to exercise suasion upon the members through their own "connections." When, however, a leader is exposed to an active organizational middle class and must have their support for leadership, he will pay for an extreme departure from their sentiments by finding a competitive leadership arising. The protest motif in the unions is closely associated with the democratic motif, which defines the leader as chosen spokesman.

If the accomodative aspect of the union's relations is important, the role will tend to select leaders who are not committed too far in the direction of militant protest. With organizational security, the criteria for leaders will change, for the administrative function, which may be defined as the reconciling of diverse pressures within a stable framework of committments, severely limits the expression of protest. The use of NLRB elections for determining affiliation of members, the importance of the legal contract, the status given internal union government by the courts, all indicate specific sanctions against irresponsibility. They also indicate a value system shared to some degree by both unions and management. For these reasons the union leader is usually a prosaic administrator, rather than the firebrand of the stereotype. However, he must still use the protest motif, for it is his basis means of production; he must be identified with the members.

In reconciling his own managerial position with his members' subordinate place in industry, he uses many tactics. He plays the role of the ordinary member in those organizational interstices where this is possible. His vocabulary and syntax, his personal appearances and interests, include those common to his members. He makes a point of personalizing relations with as many members as possible; he tries to be available in person. This is a small part of his make-up kit.

His ability to use these tactics is reinforced by his own life history; the "real union leaders" are still likely to have come from the job. Three international vice-presidents who aided in the study had all been, in their youth, ordinary manual workers in their industries. Such job experience is ordinarily required in the union constitution; the effect is to eliminate outsiders from the channels of formal power. Real leaders come from the membership and are elected by it. For the most part, the union leader shares the general point of view of his members, modified only by his different perspective on the organization and the labor movement. (This is another parallel to the race leader's role; he too shares ethnic status, identification and culture with his followers.) Thus it is difficult to separate, in these matters, the leader as leader from the leader as working man and union member.

The Union Mystique and Democratic Processes:

Much of the ideology of local union leaders can be understood with reference to their patterns of upward mobility and the insecurity of their job tenure. There is also, however, a complex of attitudes, a union mystique, which may be involved in answering the question: What do they think they are doing anyway? The manager of the most autocratic local studied stated that the union's job was "to organize the unorganized and get them wages, hours and working conditions." Another leader explained his feelings in these words.

> "I joined the union in December and they elected me president in January. And the hell of it is, I still don't know why I done it. I was comfortable, things were looking up. But you know, god damn it, a guy gets what he can make 'em pay. And for a working guy there's no chance, unless he organizes and works for his own good. And I'm sure as hell in favor of everyone improving his chances if he's got the guts to fight. If you get into a brawl you either got to hit back or else lie down and take it till the other guys get tired of sittin' on you. I never was that kind."

This basic committment to "bettering the conditions of the working guy," however, is not necessarily identified with either (1) establishing equality for minority workers or (2) maintaining democratic procedures in the locals. A minority group specialist, a Negro, tells of one committed leader.

> "My old boss was a lot of help to me in that ticklish job of selling AFL to the Negroes. He was a bastard you know, and he didn't care a damn for equality-- he didn't believe in it. But he was trade union all the way through. He'd say, 'I don't care if the Nigger is ever equal, but we can't have unions without 'em.' He was from the South you know; he'd been a molder there in a craft union and he knew Negroes could do the work. He told me about the arrangement: Negroes were only paid helper's wages but those white men were so damned lazy they let Negroes do most of the work and they got where they could do it. Then when the union called a strike the Negroes weren't members so they didn't respect the picket lines and they went right on in and did the work just as well as ever. So the old buzzard knew why you gotta have Negroes in your unions."

The functional need of unions to organize the potential labor force, though it does not imply equality for minority groups, may be used to further ethnic opportunities.

> "You know, the thing is that men who are real racist sons of bitches can still be good trade unionists, the very best. And you gotta appeal to that. A Negro machinist with a book in the IAM (he got it in Hawaii) came down to a local here and wanted a job. The dispatcher wouldn't honor his card but the Secretary said, 'Yep, you gotta do it. He's got that book, he's a member of our union and he's got to be treated as such.' Well sir, you know the dispatcher said, 'The boys will walk out' The Secretary told him, 'If they do I'll shut the damned shop down. We have a duty to that union book and anyone that holds it gets the privileges of membership. I'll pull that plant down so fast it'll make those bastards blink their eyes, if they make a ruckus.' It worked, but it don't always work so romantic."

The manager of a large industrial local, himself a Southerner, summed up the attitudes that result when "good trade unionism" is applied to the problems of ethnic workers:" Hell, I believe a nigger's black, but I believe he's human and he's got to eat!"

As for democratic processes in the union, the range is from complete autocracy to strong rank and file participation in decision-making. One labor intellectual, himself a staff member of a liberal union, gives his considered opinion: "Well, it's a hell of a thing. The unions are strictly authoritarian in structure and still they try for democratic goals." This was a common generalization by liberal labor leaders. The reaction is due, in large degree, to the impossibly high ideal of direct democracy which is common to union sympathizers, but the actuality is frequently far indeed from any sort of democratic processes. And still, the leadership of autocratic locals with no goals remotely connected with "industrial democracy" may be staunchly committed to "improving the chances of the working guys."

The ideology of union leaders then does not necessarily guarantee a committment to either the improvement of the minority workers' chances or democratic processes. Even when the individual does hold both of these aims, his own ability to make policy is ordinarily limited. His position is subject to severe constraints and his ideas are important chiefly in determining the probability of his conforming to the rules of the game" on one hand, or attempting to change them on the other. Insofar as he does conform, the situational pressures, which may be empirically determined, can be used as a predictive device for his actions. Thus it is usually safe to take the ideology of the union leader as an irrelevant or dependent factor and his place in the power structure of the local, together with the kind of local, as the chief cause of his behavior. Ideology in favor of improving the Negroe's chances is irrelevant if the leader is in no position to act on it; a sincere desire to maintain inequities based upon race will give way to sufficient pressure from management, the international, or the organized membership. If this approach is useful, the elements of the local leadership situation must be carefully examined, for the burden of explanation shifts to them.

SITUATIONAL PRESSURES ON THE LOCAL UNION LEADER

The local leader in an established local is surrounded by centers of power; he must (1) demonstrate his identification with the members (2) prove his ability to cooperate with the fraternity of labor leaders (3) accept his responsibility to management and the contract and (4) demonstrate his trustworthiness from the point of view of the international hierarchy (see Arthur Ross, (22)).

The Members:

Insofar as the leader's job is based upon the consent of his membership, he is necessarily sensitive to pressure from the members. And since the control of the membership is a basic tool in his own organizational work, he must maintain this control whatever its nature and cost. His dependence may be reduced, as in the most autocratic locals, but he still needs the members for occasional "shows of force" and, sometimes, to satisfy the international that he is the correct appointee; in the most democratic locals, however, he may be obsessed with the demands of the membership.

The International Hierarchy:

The international hierarchy always has importance for the local leader. It is supremely important in those cases where the local has lost its autonomy and is in receivership, for here the leader's job is appointive. However, even in locals with considerable autonomy, the international can help or damage a given leader through sending him support in men or money, through aiding him in internecine warfare with his rivals or through taking him up into an international job where there is more security and perhaps more pay. The international leaders, in turn, are interested in the way the local votes in conventions, the organizing record of the leadership and any tendency for a given local leadership group to "upset the apple cart" when private top level agreements with other internationals are in force.

The Management Opposite:

The management opposite the local is a factor of considerable importance to the leadership, for the union is in its nature a dependent organization. It cannot exist without management. Extreme dependence on management is evinced by locals which must make "sweetheart deals" because they lack organizational leverage; the greatest independence of direct management influence is probably in those strong locals which have a "tough management" with whom little cooperation is possible. Indirect effects of such a management are, of course, great.

Other Local Unions:

The influence of other local unions is frequently underestimated in describing the behavior of unions. Such influence may be extremely weak where strong industrial locals without competitors are concerned; in most cases, however, the local is influenced by its need to match its rivals in bargaining gains and by its reciprocal relations with allies who respect the picketlines and enforce secondary boycotts. Concern for the policy of allies is especially great among craft-type locals; they are essentially members of industrial complexes and each gains strength through helping and receiving help from others, respecting their picket lines. At the same time, these reciprocal relationships bring about considerable commitment to the partners. Such locals frequently bargain together as a unit.

The Economics of Commitment:

The importance of a specific pressure will vary according to the indispensability of that group's consent to the local leaders. Insofar as a leader has gained effective control of one of these centers of power (i. e., control for his purpose, in his field of activity) pressure from that source is reduced, limiting the number of problem areas confronted.

To appreciate the tendency toward reduction of these pressures the following possibilities should be borne in mind. (1) The members may go over to another union, answer a back to work call during a strike, or throw the leader out of his job in an election. (2) The management under contract may make a deal with another union, take full advantage of the legal framework of collective bargaining and stall indefinitely, or carefully fire the most active and useful members out of the industry. (3) Other unions in the locality may raid the local, break its strikes, or boycott its contracted parties, (4) The international hierarchy may take the union into receivership, expel the leaders from the local, fire the appointed officers, or even relinquish jurisdiction and leave the local to the mercy of rival internationals as a result of a high level deal.

These are objective possibilities and few of them apply to any one local leadership group with any urgency at one time. The leaders themselves are continually working to prevent that. It must be noted however that if the simplest motivation be attributed to the leader-- a desire to keep his job-- he is in a position of great objective insecurity compared with most executive personnel. The chief measure of his insecurity is the number of fronts on which he must be prepared to fight. Like the industrial executive opposite him at the bargaining table, he is responsible to a chain of command above and a line organization below, but unlike him he is also responsible for an electoral campaign. He must utilize the workers' antagonism to the boss yet cooperate with management, lest a lack of communication issue in strikes which are costly to union and company.

Commitments vs "Problems":

As there are pressures on the leader from several directions, and as he will attempt to accomodate to some of these, the following dichotomy results; (1) certain pressures are at a given time "under control," predictable and safe and (2) others are unstable, unpredictable and dangerous to his union and his position as leader. These are problems; the former are commitments. But relations with a given power center may shift. Thus, for example, an AFL industrial local had reached stable relations with its employers. However, the membership was stirred up by reports that a rival union was achieving better wage raises; the membership then became a problem. If, through pressure on employers, the membership is satisfied, the management groups then become problems. The leaders of the local, precipitated into the situation by a newly competing CIO local, bitterly attacked the lack of responsibility of its leaders; the static and safe had become dynamic and dangerous.

The leader is aware of both types of pressures, the stable and the dynamic: the well-structured relationships limit his area of operations and constitute a series of barriers on his actions, while he must act towards the problem relationships; they demand solution. He must be so oriented in direct proportion to the importance of problematic groups for his basic working conditions.

In considering a leader's policy towards an ethnic minority's participation in work or the local, then, it is important to know what the problems of the local union are, its basic commitments, and the probable contradictions in commitment from which new problems may be expected to issue. It is also necessary to know what kind of an issue "race" is in the local, and how it affects these basic problems or commitments. When contradictory commitments are involved, though it is not possible to predict individual behavior, it is possible to specify alternatives; the career of a race issue frequently rests upon such contradictions in commitment.

TYPES OF POWER CONFIGURATION

Leadership situations found in these locals fall into three types, based upon the source of the leadership's power, the nature of its commitments, and the kinds of problems that are apt to arise within this structure. Extreme cases are described here, for the rank order of commitment can be specified with more confidence at the extremes. Where the different pressures are more nearly equivalent, much more detailed observation is necessary. The three extreme types, international-dominated, captive, and membership-dominated locals, probably account for the majority of the locals in this sample.

International-dominated Locals:

The necessary and sufficient conditions for leadership in this type of local are simply the approval and support of the international hierarchy. There is little grass roots organization among the members; they either exist in the condition of masses, dominated by the leaders through the hiring-hall control of their jobs, or else are controlled by cadres of the leadership. Such unions frequently are able to disfranchise the members with respect to important decisions. The rank order of pressures on the leadership is (1) the international hierarchy (2) the management contracted (3) other unions in the locality and (4) the membership.

Effective pressure from the membership is a rare development, however; the leaders have no need to activate the members, for their own jobs are appointive. The international's policy is one of cooperation with employers and the union's wage policy as well as its ideology are satisfactory to the employers. As a consequence the local is more acceptable to its employers than are rival unions, and this allows organization "from the top down" to be very effective. However, the local's retreat from democratic processes has resulted, not only in freedom from effective membership pressure, but also in exposure to continuous pressure from the employers contracted.

This local leadership's concern with other unions in the locality is not limited to rivalry and jurisdictional disputes, for the local is frequently called on to aid other unions through secondary boycotts. This is due to both its strike power and the greater freedom of action the leaders have as a result of the disfranchising of their membership. However, the mutual aid relations with other unions may precipitate conflict, as in this case.

> "Well, hell, picket-lines are a mixed thing. The right to picket is one thing, but it's used without any discrimination. You have people throwing up picket-lines all the time, for everything under the sun. Now here's an example; the BA of one of the metal trades unions throws a line up around Solar Fan Company because he don't like the manager of the company. Are we going to call our members off of there because this son of a bitch doesn't like a guy and lose our members fifteen dollars a day until this guy gets his grudge out?
> We want to have some say about that picket line, and when and why it's there, before we're going to honor it irrespective...."

Such a local is committed to ally unions, but its commitments conflict with its debts to management the other union leaders, finding they cannot count on support "irrespective," label the local a company union. This bad name is resented by the local's leaders, for they are a part of the fraternity of labor union leaders, yet commitment to their employers is a necessary condition for keeping their jobs and their local operating under these circumstances.

Such conflicts also occur between the demands of the international hierarchy and those of organizational allies. One such example occurred during the course of the study. The local broke an organizing strike among very low level workers by passing through their picket lines. There was supposed to have been a telegram from the international telling them to honor their contracts. When asked about it, the officers explained: "The state senator in that district was for us on this damned bill(which would have outlawed the secondary boycott) and we had to have his vote in committee." Yet the officers of this local, which effectively broke the strike of the ally union, contributed over $1,000. in strike aid to the losing union.

The leaders of international-dominated locals are thus not free of problems arising out of contradictions in commitment. The minimal attention to the members as participants plus the employer orientation in collective bargaining also results in some strain; employers, however, are higher on the rank order for, with their cooperation the leaders can "take care of their members" and also repress any rebellious stirring in the rank and file. Thus the international's directives may be followed. The reactions of the members is problematical. One leader assayed them as follows.

> "The members have discovered they can't do a damned thing about it. They're tied hand and foot. But there's no question that the members feel considerable confidence in the International. It's like a big business, that handles one commodity, labor.
>
> "Sure these guys want to organize. The more you organize, the bigger your stockpile of commodities, the more power and prestige your business has. And what are wages and conditions but prices for the commodity? It's big business and it's run on big business lines.
>
> "Have you been in their public relations department? Well, I've been in Louis B. Mayer's and I'll tell you it looks shabby besides that set-up."

Without the cooperation of the employers, however, the leaders would have to activate the membership; this would not only strain the resources of a staff long accustomed to ignoring the wishes of the members, but would also have the effect of transforming the stable relation with the membership into a dynamic one, a problem. This would be followed by a similar change in relations with employers. Such a development would in turn have the effect of "bringing the international down on the local." The leaders would probably be dismissed and a new international representative would come in.

Captive Locals:

The rank order of pressure on the leadership here is as follows: (1) powerful allied unions and the international hierarchy (2) management and (3) the members. Concern with other unions is closely associated with concern for the international hierarchy's decisions; management is next, the members a poor fourth. (Reference here is not to the leadership's sympathy or values, but to those pressures which must be taken into account.) Such unions probably do not amount to a large percentage of the total; since, however, they usually organize low status, unskilled workers, they have a particular importance for ethnic minorities. Locals of this type in the sample were preponderantly Negro and Mexican in membership composition.

The strike power of the local is slight, due to the dispensability of the function, and the local's bargaining power derives chiefly from its relations with other unions. These are made more secure through amicable relationships at a higher level, between the internationals. Such relationships, however, strengthen the local leaders' commitments to both centers of power-- their own international and the allied internationals.

> "You know we have those operators in our union. Well, out in the Valley our contract gives us a five hour day and it's a seven day week, so they have a thirty-five hour week. Now here in L. A. we don't have that, but we figured we were going to get it.
>
> "Well, we operated with a joint contract in those plants. The (powerful ally) union got a contract that they liked, so they proceeded to high-hand it, making it a five year contract. Well honestly, Jones (the local's top leader) blew up. He couldn't take it.
>
> "Then the top man of their international came down and talked with Jones. He said, 'You'll take it whether you like it or not. If that five hour day bothers you, we'll see that it is discontinued in the Valley.' Then he got in touch with our International President, and told him Jones was giving trouble. Our President wired Jones to take it and quit beefing."

The international hierarchy sees to it that the local leadership gets along with other significant unions in the area, while the importance of the ally union is usually so great that the local officer is rarely in any position to defy his ally even if he wishes to. Jones, whose reaction to pressure is described above, remarked, concerning his relations with another powerful ally:

> "We had our contract opened early this year, you know. The reason is that we would have been in the position of getting two cents more than the (ally union). Common laborers! Well, you can imagine the uproar there would have been if we'd get more wages than them. Of course we've been fighting for parity for a long time and I think that's a sound position. But good God, we can't afford to go <u>over</u> them. And with our regular ten per cent we would have done it.
> "If we'd have got that two cents, our employers would all have felt like throwing our union out, to stop the unpleasantness they'd be in for!"

The fact that this local does not own its means of production, its effective strike power, limits its relations with management also. Such a local is frequently involved in joint negotiations with stronger internationals <u>vis à vis</u> management groups; in these cases the union's weight is apt to be slight in the bargaining process. When the local was considering a contract with a major employer, the BA described the terms to the members in great detail (he is an outstanding labor liberal) and concluded: "Of course we'll have to go along with the other locals in any case, because here are all of these big, powerful, organizations and we amount to a very small part of the bargaining group."

Outside the areas where the union is firmly committed to policy made by others the officers can develop a degree of independence; this comes about through personal relations with important individuals in the allied unions and in management. Such influence should not be confused with power; it has no base in organizational strength. The leaders are able, however, to secure greater cooperation, within the limits of the power relationship, than would be expected if these informal, person to person bonds were not present. The union's leaders may thus have an influence on its allies as well as management, but the local's power of coercion is very limited and derived chiefly from ties with those whose strikes can damage the enemy.

Important decisions in the local are made by the staff and the leaders of other unions; the membership, willy-nilly, becomes a plebiscitary body, in Herberg's phrase (18). The more the local's strength rests upon these personal relations noted above, the more indispensable does the incumbent leadership become. Such a local simply cannot stay in business unless it gets along with its allies. The negotiating committee is described by one BA.

> "Well, they're chosen by appointment of the President, who's elected. Of course they're not really negotiators. They are the link between the negotiators-- the BA's-- and the actual membership. They help to reconcile the members to the course the negotiations take and help them to make up their mind in a more informed way."

This local had gone out on strike with its powerful allies in the recent past and the strike had been broken--with most of the local's members' jobs taken by "scabs" (or replacements). The Business Manager considering the strike at some length, said:

> "We were one of the locals that got the full force of that strike-- all those six long months. We had to go back and negotiate an entrance. It was hard to take but there was nothing else for it. When you're licked, you're licked.
>
> "Of course I had told those guys (leaders of other unions) we were crazy to go out, that the employers wanted a strike. But they wouldn't listen. How could *I* tell them?"

There is also conflict between the management contracted and the demands of other, allied unions. The local had organized its workers in one industry one hundred per cent and was ready to accept the terms management offered. However the powerful union, also parties to the contract, insisted on a union-shop clause in the contract-- and the weak local had to go along with a demand that would not profit its own organizing efforts. An officer concluded: "Those guys can't organize their own men, so they have to get a union-shop contract. We *have* our men, damn it, and still we get screwed."

In summary, locals which approximate this configuration of pressures are dependent for their existence upon factors which neither the leaders, the members, nor the management opposite can control, and of which the latter two groups are usually unaware. Such locals tend to have a heavy concentration of Negro and Mexican members and the leaders are "liberal" on the race issue. Their ability to change the ethnic *status quo* is limited by the above considerations.

Membership-dominated Locals:

Locals which are oriented towards the membership as a source of strength are those in which the leadership group has job tenure and control of strike power through control of the members. In such a local the rank order of pressures is (1) the members (2) the management opposite (3) the international hierarchy and (4) the other locals in the area. Office depends upon election in these locals and strike power depends upon mobilizing the membership in crises. Management is a constant concern, for these are management groups who compete for the control of the members. Other unions are hardly important, for these locals are preponderently industrial in nature and the secondary boycott is relatively ineffectual.

The danger areas for the leadership in such locals are then (1) the formation of rival cadres and factions (2) the "union busting" management and (3) if the local leaders are weak, the international hierarchy. The strongest leadership groups are those which effectively organize and control their members: they have little to fear from any of these centers. Their chief source of conflict is the basic one between accommodation and protest in their bargaining with management. Too strong a commitment either way will allow new competitors to arise from the membership; this is one reason for the building of machines.

Some notion of the complexities of leadership in these locals is gained through considering one industrial local. It is made up of several large plants, organized in plant units. Each plant has an organized and self-conscious rank and file. There is a paid staff which is elected by the members, and the officers necessarily keep in touch with the executive board and the rank and file.

In this local management exerts considerable pressure on the leaders, for the members can affect the existence and strength of the local. Management and local are in continual competition for the members' allegiance. And, since this is true, management uses issues internal to the union in combating the leadership's hold on the members. The ethnic issue is one obvious weapon against the leadership, for the union has a heavy ethnic contingent in its membership. There is a strong schism on ethnic lines, and, like any serious and continuing division among the members, it is useful to management.

Because of the relative weakness of the local organizationally, the leaders are dependent upon the international hierarchy. The international had a "watch dog" representative in the local at the time of the study and the leader had no recourse but to cooperate; had he a stronger hold upon his members and hence upon his management groups, he would have been a "power" in the International.

One probable contradiction faced by such a leadership group is that between commitment to factions in the local on one hand and working arrangements with management on the other. When, in addition, the leader must depend on the factions and they side with management, something is likely to give. This is continually occurring in the local; as is obvious from the above discussion, the leader has fewer stable conditions and more problems then do leaders in the other power situations. What frequently results is an uneasy compromise between two opposing pressures, with neither of the indispensable relations stabilized. In this local the international's policy of non-discrimination against Mexicans and Negroes hindered the immediate development of local strength, both with respect to factions in the local and relations with management. Yet it had considerable effect in creating positive support for the union and its leaders among Mexican and Negro members.

Should a leader in this position try to solve his problem by capturing the membership, leaving himself free to deal with management from a position of strength, he will run against other limits. Although there is always a tendency towards machine control in these locals, so long as the union must have the consent of the members the machines are far from perfect. In the local described, the need for the consent of the membership is great indeed; there are no union-shop contracts, due to the power of management, and the state of the local organization is perennially in doubt.

Locals that are captured by their staff and dominated by their international hierarchy are at the mercy of the international's executive board; their leaders are appointed. Locals dominated by other internationals are dependent upon them for their own existence as organizations, and have leadership groups closely controlled from above. Membership-dominated locals are forced, by the nature of their hold on members and employers (and hence on organizational existence) to be continually aware of the interests and the political articulation of the membership. The orientation of leaders in these locals towards specific issues can be understood only in terms of such basic pressures. While an individual leader may refuse to recognize these limits, unless he can change the organization's structure and his basis for tenure he violates the limits at the expense of his job or his local.

SUMMARY: THE UNION LEADER AND HIS CAGE OF PRESSURES

It is the number of forces and the inherent conflicts between them which cause labor leaders to work continually at stabilizing vital relationships. The general strategy is not to abolish opposing pressures (this is usually impossible) but rather to seek accommodation. Agreement reduces the objective insecurity for each party and, at the same time, commits each party. It narrows the range of alternatives and increases predictability. However, in stabilizing these pressures the leader commits himself to specific behavior, becoming "the international's hatchet man," "a friend of the Teamsters," or, at the other extreme, "a rank and file rabble-rouser" or "a friend of the Negroes." The more necessary such commitments are for the leader's security and the local's strength, the less likely their violation. These conditions, in turn, will generate the three typical configurations of commitment.

With such commitments, personal values make very little difference in the leader's actions. Thus the Negro leader who was responsible to a mixed membership may have been subjectively committed to a Fair Employment Practices Program, yet the combined strength of his commitments to the organized white faction in his local and to his contracted management groups resulted in his helping to sabotage the program. The union leader, threatened and insecure, fights toward autonomy, but he stops halfway with accommodation.

CHAPTER V

THE ASSOCIATIONAL BASIS OF UNION POLITICAL STRUCTURE

The situation of the local union leader can be derived from the nature of his commitments, translated as the necessary conditions for keeping his job. Commitments, in turn, may be traced to the organizational strategies and necessities of the local union. The union exists only as a structure which coordinates and controls the behavior of workers primarily occupied with jobs in the economic sector of the society. Therefore, the associational patterns resulting from the organization of work in contemporary society are crucial for union power and structure. Though these patterns do not force a "democratic" or "authoritarian" control system on a local, they narrow the limits and set the degrees of freedom.

The legitimation of power and the fact of power for any local union derive from the four sources of pressure described as encircling the labor leader: members, management, the international, the allied locals. Each source transfers strength in a different fashion to the specific leader and to the organization. The membership supports the leader by its voting, and by its solidary action. Whether this support results in a commitment on the leader's part, making him their representative, is an open question which can only be answered through analyzing specific empirical types of locals.

This chapter will be concerned with the various forms of political articulation found in union electorates; the political stratification of those electorates, and the associational bases of different political systems in the work groups of the union members.

POLITICAL ARTICULATION OF THE UNION ELECTORATE

The most striking aspect of the attendance at Special Election meetings is the tremendous increase over participation at the General Membership meetings of the local. On the average, attendance increases four or five times over, so that most locals have more than half of the members voting. These members, however, may come from various widely separated plants and most of them are not actives; they come out only for issues which are high in the order of importance to them, as workers on the job, particularly contract issues and the election of the leaders who negotiate contracts. Such members are an unpredictable element in the political system of the local; in general, the officers themselves are braced for a surprise when an election is in the offing. (Thus the naive statement of one business agent in a report to the Central Labor Council: "I'm sure you will all be glad to know that our officers have all come safely through another election!") Variation in the exposure of the voting members to the union organization is a central factor in the political system of the local.

A "winning majority" of the voters has little regular contact with the union in the hall. This majority expresses the feelings and opinions formulated from on-the-job experience (or lack of experience) of the local organization, articulated perhaps through on-the-job meetings of the plant units or channelled through gossip. The majority's information is likely to be less pertinent to the "localwide" situation than is that of the actives, and relationships with the existing set of officers as well as with the oppositions are looser.

The segmental participation of most voters makes manipulation probable; they are unacquainted with the month-to-month operation of the local and the record of the incumbents. They are logical targets for interpretation of the election; it can be filled with content for them in one way or another. It may, for example, be turned into a struggle along ethnic lines, or it may be interpreted as a struggle against a "sold out" set of officers (one side) or a "foreign, union-busting outift" (the opposing side).

How does such interpretation come about? There are two basic forms of association between union members-- on the job and in the union hall. On-the-job campaigning, "talking up" an issue or candidate, is usually coordinated with some influence in the hall meetings, since the same small number of people tend to be protagonists in both fields. However, on-the-job campaigning makes use of informal networks of association in the plants; a very popular key man in a given plant may very quickly attract wide support, though he has not been an active heretofore. When a vote is heavy it usually indicates that the campaign has mobilized many such informal leaders. According to a veteran leader, a virtual two-party system is necessary to bring out a heavy vote (23).

> "Well, he has experienced opposition, people who've been in office themselves and know what they're doing. In the election before last he won by seventy votes out of 3,000 cast (in a local with 5,000 members). This time he did better, winning by a large margin, but there was still over 3,000 votes this time, too. That's damned unusual. What happened was that they really got out and worked, canvassing the membership you know. Because you don't get a vote out in a week-- you have to work at it, on the job and at meetings, for months. And in this

case, both sides did just that."

If the incumbents have "done a good job and got our boys the going rate" the official slate, made up of incumbents with whatever substitutions are necessary due to resignations, will usually carry in an almost automatic fashion. And, even when there is violent opposition as in the case above, the incumbent in a paid, full-time staff position has a considerable advantage over the opposition. His work allows for greater mobility and contact with the members at important points: he is, in effect, paid by the local for campaigning. The same officer quoted above continued:

> "He looked after the interests of the membership much better last term(after the close election, e.g.) that's why he won. He has also got out and worked with the business agents instead of waiting around here in the office. All of this pays off."

The incumbent has the further advantage of access to the formal structure of the local itself, including not only a favorable position to influence hall meetings and publications, but also the chance to appoint and influence the stewards in many locals. Some notion of how this works may be found in the remarks of a former business agent.

> "Naw, I don't like political machines. They're dangerous. You're always getting into trouble; the boys get ambitious. Now when I had the old local, I would phone the boys and get twenty or thirty on my side, so I'd have the votes when an issue came up. But I got too busy for that. It's hard to take all day for that sort of thing. And when you're so busy, you appoint your stewards and you just naturally expect them to go down the line for you on a vote. But they all get ambitious."

Such influence is not one-way; the stewards in turn have the "inside track" to the staff of the local. The steward who brings a friend in to the office to ask about the prospects for his getting a job through the union is likely to be listened to and, if possible, helped.

Permanent Voting Blocs: Cadres and Factions:

This brings the discussion to a consideration of the permanent voting groups in the locals. These may be classified in two types, the cadres and the factions. As these terms are sometimes used with other denotations, these definitions are intended; a faction is a group held together by similar interests with regard to a given issue; a cadre is a group whose coordinated political behavior is the result of organizational bonds for which the specific issue is not important.

Cadres:

These differ from factions, not only in the irrelevance of particular issues, but also in the degree of manipulability to which the members are subject from the leaders. An operational distinction between cadre and faction might be made on the basis of the consistency of voting patterns. The cadre can be expected to vote together on all issues of importance, though its vote on one issue may be logically inconsistent with that on another. The faction, however, though united in respect to given issues, and voting consistently with respect to these issues, can be expected to scatter its vote and divide on other important issues which are not a common ground for cooperation. This points back to the basis for organization; the line of authority in the cadre is universal (in the political system of the local) and is unidirectional. Whether the leaders derive their position from status in an outside group or from their official position in the local, the leaders determine behavior for the entire cadre. The faction, however, is a looser and more informal type of association. As a faction becomes highly organized and manipulable, it moves toward the condition of a cadre. In other words, the cadre is group oriented, the faction, issues oriented.

The machines indicated by the informant quoted above are probably the most common form of cadre in the locals; another is the fraction-- the group within a union which has superordinate interests in some outside organization of which it is a part. Communist Party fractions are classic examples of this type of cadre and racketeers in unions are another type.

An official-dominated cadre is described by an officer in a large local union:

> (Question: Isn't the problem of control difficult in the locals with so many transients among the members?)
> "A hard local to handle? Don't you believe it. Those are the easiest locals of all. Why? Turnover. Most of the guys don't stick around long enough to gang up. And you can run it with the cadre-- that's all there is to it. The cadre is the union.
> "That's certainly true of us, too. You take the (casual laborers), our equivalent of those guys you mentioned, they got a cadre there that runs our entire local. It's simple. They're Sam's boys. No, you don't even have to give 'em much pay for it."
> (Question: How is the cadre kept in line?)
> "Well, you don't even have to give them a better job--

> just a regular job. If they're out in one place where they work, you get 'em another place. If they get drunk a couple times, they can still work anyhow. This kind of job security will buy 'em."

It is probable that in such a local the cadre actually selects the most irresponsible elements in the membership and upon this basis the government of the union is carried on.

The fraction as a cadre is described in the following statement made by an opposition leader from a Communist dominated local.

> "Well, there are about forty active party members, but they are disciplined and they work hard. If we try to get a leaflet out, it takes us a week. But if they want one out they call those guys off their jobs--the union makes it OK --and they have them at every plant in a couple hours. And then, they have guys from outside the union, too, who can be borrowed.
>
> "The dispatcher is a colored guy and eight-tenths of the placements now are Negroes and this strengthens the cadre. The Mexicans are getting mad. Usually though they don't come out to meetings too well and the Negroes with a CP member as a party whip come in a block. The whip gets up and makes them vote together; since he's chief steward at the plant, it works. The dispatcher is also the chairman at the meetings, and he refuses to let the opposition speak-- he discriminates against us."

In this case the Party cadre is almost identical with the official cadre which controls the structure of the local.

Factions:

These are groups organized on the basis of issues; they may be relatively permanent or they may be quite temporary. The latter kind of issue is exemplified in the chronic question, "How militant can we be in the negotiations?" Of the more permanent issues, ethnic issues are prominent. Such issues have an obvious utility in a mixed local, particularly since the Mexican or Negro workers are apt to be concentrated in particular job-levels, where interests may conflict with those on other jobs. In such a case ethnic differences coincide with skill and status differences. Further, ethnic issues can be used to mobilize strength for many purposes (as the leader quoted above used "discrimination against Mexicans" to fight the officers). The ethnic issue has the further advantage of permanence--it allows for continuity in the organization built upon it (and such an organization may become a cadre). The ethnic issue may become "localwide"; it is more apt to be centered in specific plants and to affect the local through these plants' work forces.

"The majority of the Negroes are in one plant. Well, I'll tell you, working conditions there are so low nobody else would work there. The chief steward has them really under control and has the management scared too."

A leader in another local with ethnic factions reported:

"We just had a Christmas party and we teamed up with the Mine, Mill and Smelters. Oh, we used the same hall and shared expenses. All of the locals went along fine, except that one local. But they simply raised hell and took no part in it, because the party was interracial. Their leadership, which uses race baiting to stay in office, was dead-set against it. Then another thing: when they sent out that southern extradition order, our leader (a Negro) let them use his name on the petition (against extradition). You know, while he was off to the international convention, those guys in that local started a strong move to impeach him! For playing footsie with the Communists!"

The following is a summary of a temporary ethnic faction which arose in a large one-job laborers' local.

"Up until this year the different races came out about proportionally to our elections, but this year we had a Negro guy run on a race ticket-- just plain Negro, nothing else for anybody else. And you know, the Mexicans and the whites really came out-- the most whites I've ever seen I guess. The Negroes, they didn't like it on the whole; many didn't come for that reason I think. Few voted for him. But usually you get a fairly average proportion, about the same for each group. Occasionally we have a Mexican guy try it on his being a Mexican. He can get a lot of support just because of those big families they have, but this sort of thing doesn't usually work."

Factions arise when the perennial questions of special assessments and dues raises come up; on such issues new factions will form and old ones will split and merge. Cadres, however, will behave as units.

Machine Democracy:

It is a part of the ideology of voluntary organizations to express hostility towards cliques and cliqueishness, and unions are not exceptions. Caroline Rose has documented this in a study of union stewards in Detroit (31). Such hostility may, of course, be a disguise for a general antagonism to opposition. It must be observed, however, that conflict between two or more evenly matched factions can make the course of a local's actions very irregular, while the struggle for partisan advantage may be disadvantageous to the membership as a whole. The Teamster official who said "Democracy is a damned popularity contest that interferes with the organizing" was making a general statement that finds considerable covert agreement among the officers of many diverse locals.

Illustrating the conflict between "popularity contest" and "the organizing" is the following anecdote.

> "He got us a damned good contract compared to what we'd had before and he would go down the line for you with the Company. But you'd oughta heard those guys grouse. The damned fools didn't know what they'd got. Then, when he came up for election, he lost out to Schmidt.
>
> "Now Schmidt is a very agreeable guy, but the only thing he would be good for is just one job-- a Greeter. He'd make a fine Greeter, smiles and all!"
>
> (Question: How did the Manager lose out?)
>
> "Oh hell, he was out negotiating the contract and so tied up he couldn't do anything. Meanwhile Schmidt and a lot of guys for him were glad-handing everyone. And the Manager didn't work at building him up a caucus; he figured if he'd do a good job the guys would appreciate it. Instead, they threw him out.
>
> "Do you know, the local actually voted to pay him to go on working for them, negotiating that contract, for months after they defeated him? They knew he was a good man!"

The labor union, whose formal constitution is much like that of the United States, must return for its validation to the membership. Without the development of the faction or the cadre the union must suspend its constitution (which is the case in the local of the Teamster leader quoted earlier) or hamper the paid staff seriously in the performance of its duties. The internal organization of the members, in cliques, caucuses, cadres and factions, provides a certain degree of security and predictability for the elected staff. This is analagous to the function of the political party in a democracy. The internal organization may, of course, eventuate in complete dominance of the local by a few individuals; on the other hand, it may allow for the development of strong, consistent pressures on the officers which force them to consider the interests of at least a part of the membership. These same pressures will then give the staff political strength to act in accordance with membership interests. The question is not the desirability of internal subgroups within the unions (for they are inevitable) but the conditions under which these groups function as two-way channels for relations with the membership as a whole.

VARIETIES OF UNION POLITICAL STRUCTURE

Union members may be differentiated into three classes with respect to their participation in the local's political structure -- the professional leaders, the "actives," and the rank and file. One useful way to divide the locals in the sample is by the relative importance of these different classes in the control of the local.

A clear type is the local mentioned earlier, whose organizational meetings are packed with a cadre of workers from the lower ranks. The cadre in turn is controlled by the staff which, in short, elects itself. In such a local the decision making is a monopoly of the staff, the executive board is subservient and the actives are either part of the cadre or doomed to futile opposition. Political difficulties arise for the staff only when another cadre is formed within the local, usually in connection with a split in the top leadership.

In another type of local which appeared several times in this sample, the executive board is itself made up of staff members without rank and file representation; the dominant leader controls the board through his personal sway over the members. This leader is a fiery orator with great personal charisma; he appoints his board, which becomes his cadre. There can be little effective pressure from the board, caught between the leader's authority on one hand and the membership he controls on the other. So little respect had this individual for his executive board that he retires to his own offices during the board meetings. He communicates with the board through a two-way public address system; his impressive speaking voice has something of the effect of a *deus ex machina* upon the humble President, Vice-President, Trustees and other members.

Finally, a number of locals had executive boards elected by the various plants. Each board member had his own plant constituency, his independent base of power; the executive board as a whole had considerable braking effect upon the staff. Each member was responsible to his plant constituency and derived his power from them.

With a similar formal constitution and ideology, these three locals have control systems varying so widely that the first might well be called machine rule, the second, charismatic dictatorship, the third, democratic decentralization. In explaining this variation, the single factor which indicates most accurately the nature of local government is the effective independent power of the actives, the participating rank and file. Their status determines the degree of reciprocity between leaders and led the relation between control and consent.

In labor unions, as in all organizations, there is apt to be considerable social distance between the rank and file members and the small group of highly committed top leaders. This condition cannot be abolished by (1) making the entire rank and file into leaders or (2) somehow constraining the leadership to be at the same time "top dogs" and "bottom dogs." Neither the nature of participation in segmental groups (in the first case) nor the necessities of leadership (in the second) will allow these "democratic solutions." The situation is permanent, for organizations demand differentiation of roles and someone must be in the leadership role.

The Organizational Middle Class:

When democratic, or reciprocal, control processes are at work, they usually turn out to rest upon the activity of a small minority of members, whose function is that of mediating between the top leaders and the mass of members. This is the "organizational middle class." (The term has no connection with socio-economic class, of course.) It is a self-selected group of representatives, members who have some communication among themselves, as well as access to both the top leadership and the rank and file. In the locals, contact with the rank and file is assured by continued work on the job; contact with the top leaders comes only through the formal structure of the local.

This middle group has interests which are separate from those of the staff, though with the staff they share a concern for the organization as a whole. Their information is sufficient to allow some understanding of the staff's actions and policy, but their information also extends to the general thinking and feeling of the masses of members whom they represent. Their influence is, finally, based upon neither control of the central administration of the local nor upon outside forces; it stems from persuasion and consent, the informal processes that come into play at the level of the job.

The effects of such a group are many and varied. One

general consequence may be the diffusion through the membership of a more realistic knowledge of the staff's goals and the local's problems, without an accompanying commitment to the staff's goals. At the same time the organizational middle class is in a position to enforce the staff's commitment to the interests of the members as a whole, rather than to those of the staff (for all leaders come in time to confuse their own careers with that of their organizations). Perhaps their most primitive function is to keep the leaders honest.

Where an organizational middle class exists in the locals, the actives are neither merged with the paid leadership, on the one hand, nor collapsed into the organizational masses on the other. They constitute an effective force, restraining and constraining the top leadership's actions.

There are certain structural conditions which make this state of affairs more likely; these are, in turn, related to the *modus vivendi* of the total organization with its institutional environment. The three locals described above are neither operated by demons (in the first two cases) nor paragons of virtue (in the third). They are, however, different kinds of locals, and they organize different kinds of job structures.

JOB STRUCTURE AND POWER STRUCTURE

The source of union power is the ability of the organization to bind men into a stable group, which may then be controlled in relations with the employer (26). In this primitive sense the union depends upon the consent of the members and this is frequently what is meant when the inherent democracy of labor unions is discussed. However, no democratic *processes* are implied beyond the primitive fact of dependency, for men may be controlled in numerous ways.

There are differing degrees of freedom for those who must consent. In the case of the worker, possible alternatives to joining a given local may range from "no job" in one situation to a "no union" vote in another. The width of his range of choice depends upon the effective strength of the union-- the degree to which it controls job opportunities. In the building trades in Los Angeles it is very difficult to work without a union card; in certain large mass industries it was once almost as difficult to work *with* a union card. The range of freedom of choice for the member must be known, in considering the degree of consent necessary to the local. The difference between the building trades and weak industrial locals calls attention to variation in the social structure of the job. One significant difference between the two types of locals lies in the nature of the work group, for on-the-job association of the members provides a very basic set of limits within which the union organization takes shape. The work group, a result of technological operations and social organization in an area of work, is relatively non-controllable by any given local. It is a constant condition for social interaction, allowing certain types of power to be generated and setting certain limits to any association the union can organize and control.

Thus work organized on craft lines is work that is carried on by relatively small groups of workers and it is frequently intermittent in character, so that the work group is very fluid. Work organized by industrial locals is carried on by large groups of workers; it is continuous and the work group is relatively stable.

The two recurring patterns in this sample of local unions are (1) those locals organizing small, fluid work groups, which perform a single kind of job and (2) those organizing large, stable work groups, which operate an entire plant through highly "rationalized" patterns, and consequently include workers in many kinds of jobs. The type of relationship between union and member differs with the nature of the work group.

LOCALS ORGANIZING SMALL, FLUID, WORK GROUPS

These locals may be divided into those which have considerable independent strike power and those which do not. Of the first category, the conventional craft unions are usually considered the best example. Their strike power, based upon their monopoly of essential techniques, is very great. Unions such as carpenters' locals have only to withdraw from the work to enforce their demands. With the support of other members of the local (more or less automatic, due to the hiring-hall system) and of other unions in the craft-complex who respect their picket lines, they can quickly bring an individual employer to consider changing his ways.

However, certain other unions are very powerful though they do not monopolize any craft. It is their position in the flow of work which is crucial. Since they do not monopolize skill, they must prevent the entry of competing labor forces into their jobs when they go on strike. In locals such as those of the Longshoremen and the Teamsters, the basic fact that withdrawal is not enough to damage the employer forces the union to use suasion, moral or physical, to prevent replacement by non-union workers. If this can be done the union is powerful indeed.

Other locals have neither a craft nor a crucial position in the work flow from which to generate strike power. The one-job unions in this sample are frequently in this situation. In such locals, where replacements are plentiful and the function is not critical, there is a continual reliance upon support from other unions through use of the picket line, secondary boycott, and the "unfair list." It is not surprising that such locals participate with unusual vigour in the Central Labor Council; they cannot operate in isolation from their allies with stronger jurisdictions.

Size of the Work Group and the Economics of Organizing:

Unions based upon small, fluid work groups, have distinctive problems in organizing and distinctive solutions. Such unions are faced with widely scattered work groups having little communication between them. There is first the sheer difficulty of locating and communicating with the members; second, the overwhelming job of writing thousands of contracts at a few members each. Few large permanent aggregations justify a great expenditure of effort in the jurisdiction to be organized. A staff member in such a local discussed the problem.

> "Walter's work is more general-- trouble shooting and organizing. He's one hell of a fine organizer. I heard the Chief tell him-- and I thought it was a joke-- 'Walter, you have <u>got</u> to slow down on organizing. It takes too damned <u>long</u> to write contracts. We're three months behind already.' Well, damn it, he wasn't joking! It's really true; you know the job Jake organized? Well, by God, it's took him three weeks on that one contract-- and it's only fifteen people."

The simplest solution is frequently that of promoting an employers' association. The same informant continued:

> "Now Abe is a smart guy. He was organizing out in the Valley, and he persuaded an idiot out there (a real idiot, the kind that suddenly in the middle of a conversation makes a face and goes 'Bow Wow!') to form a Valley contractor's association. So we could write only one contract for all of them. Well, this fool does this and gets us four members for his association, and what do you know! At the first meeting they voted him out as President. The outfit has seven or eight employers now, thirty some odd men; a tidy contract!"

Some notion may be gotten of the choices available to employers and workers in one craft complex from the following case.

> A worker came into the office of a large craft union with the card of some contractor and said, "I want to work for this guy; what do I do?"
> The business agent checked a file, then phoned the Building Trades Joint Council (an organization of craft unions and union contractors) then said, "The outfit is not a union shop. You'll have to tell him to come down here and sign up." The member said, "OK, I'll phone him. Can I use your phone?" Instead, he went outside to phone.
> Later the contractor called the BA, who reported the man had said "Do I have to sign a union shop agreement to get any workers? Isn't this America?" And the BA said he had replied, "Sure, this is America, but America is an organization and you have certain rights and laws to respect. You have to sign or you just don't get any men at all." The fellow had then said, "Alright, if that's what has to be done," and to this the BA had replied, "We've got it in our union-shop contract that our men will not break our contract with the thousand other employers we have got contracts with here in the County."

When, however, the union has no skill monopoly, it is driven to other expedients. Since the members are difficult to organize and can be easily replaced by the employer if they strike, the professional picket and the secondary boycott become very important.

> "So they call us strictly a "goon" outfit, with the exception of us two guys-- a goon outift and nothing but. Well, I guess that's about right, but you've got to understand our organizing situation. So many of these jobs are little outfits, run down, one man owns them, and its really tough on the workers. So most of our guys are chosen for brawn-- they got to be."

The importance of violence is commonly either underrated or grossly exaggerated in describing union organizing. It must be realized that violence is localized and, also, is usually two way.

> "Look at this Sally Slater deal-- four months of it. I was out there one morning-- God it was rough. The minute your picket line got down to less than four guys, a couple thugs would rush out of the plant gate in a car and beat hell out of some of you! Even girls and old women too. It made no difference to those boys."

Such violence figures largely in the organizing attempts of locals whose jurisdiction involves small, isolated and technologically weak work groups.

When the local is organizing a crucial work force, such as Longshoremen or Teamsters, it is only necessary to prevent any replacements for the struck workers (and to prevent the workers' returning) in order to exercise sufficient pressure on the employer. When, however, the local has no independent strike power it must have support from other unions.

> "Well, we don't organize the people from the bottom; we organize from the top. You can do that, with secondary boycotts. That's how we organized (a large chain) last year. We had their truck drivers and we had their _____s, so they had to organize their own workers for us. Which they did. Even so, we didn't win the first election; so the boss said 'Gimme those blue cards!' I did, and he signed 'em up at a big meeting they called. Of course they didn't have to go, but they were told to by the Company on the company bulletin boards and so they went.
> "We've about got to the bottom of the barrel though, with the boycott and the picket line."
> (Question: Do you use the NLRB elections?)
> "No sir, we never use it unless we're forced to. We resist it when management wants it. We want our John L. Lewis clause in there, so we can strike when we need to."

Such locals must, of course, maintain working agreements with the unions controlling the workers mentioned, if they are to succeed in their strikes.

Status and Power of the Leaders:

The problems facing these locals and the solutions they have evolved result in certain very common patterns of internal union relationships. Two separate but related aspects will be discussed; (1) the union member--staff relationship and (2) the political basis of the top leadership.

One consequence of the scattered nature of the small work groups is that the union must continually patrol its jobs. In such a local the paid staff and the membership are both mobile. The most constant expression of the union is the appearance of the business agent, known to the members at a new job manned by a newly assorted crew, under a superintendent or foreman who may be known to none of them. The BA appears for very specific purposes; to assure the union's control over the conditions of work including who works-- whether the crew is all union. In such a service role the BA, expressing the official power of the union, tends to become the union, to both employers and members, just as an individual policeman is sometimes treated as the law.

As one good trade unionist in such a local remarked:

> "You know, its a damned funny thing. To us guys in this union the BA's are untouchable. We see them as union policemen, come out to see if everyone has a card and has paid his dues. Then too, he's a friend of the Boss and he goes in to have coffee and beer with *him*."

There is a strong tendency for such business agents to see themselves in an analagous position to that of management *vis à vis* the members. Both are supervisors and administrators with white collar status. The manager of one large local said, upbraiding his staff of BA's, "The members never see you. You go first thing to the Boss's office. But they say among themselves, 'Who the Hell does he think pays his salary-- the Boss, or us?' "

The hiring hall as the source of jobs is made necessary by the scatter and fluidity of the work force but the consequent organization of the employers tends to reinforce the officer-member relationship described. Given the most favorable circumstances, e.g., straight "down the board" or unbiased selection of men for jobs, the officials are still important persons to each member. The importance of work opportunities in such fluctuating labor markets as building construction or transportation makes the individual's trip to the hall his most important exposure to the union.

Ordinarily, however, straight down the board selection is not observed, for a number of reasons. The employer orientation, incident to the emphasis on union employers rather than union workers, generally carries many formal safeguards for the employer. The skill of the workers, the satisfaction with performance clauses, may be powerful discriminating devices, especially as applied to ethnic minorities. One BA explained the unemployment of Negroes in his trade, where they are traditionally proficient, in these terms: "The contractors don't hire them because they *know* the white guys are better mechanics."

Unions also frequently allow crew selection to the foreman, who is himself chosen by the contractor; the informal selective processes at work here further emphasize the importance of the paid staff as men of power, rather than underlining the union rules as powerful norms. In such locals one sees Negroes standing around the door of the BA's office half a day while men are sent out on jobs and being told, when they approach hat-in hand, "Get away and stop bothering me. I tell you there's nothing doing." The specific attitudes of individual office holders in such a local are more likely to be determinants in the hiring process than in locals where control of the jobs is shared with other forces-- whether management or union in origin.

In summary, the disproportionate power and status of the union official relative to any given member is emphasized in these locals. His power is essentially one of administration and regulation-- policing the contract, as it is significantly called. Such locals are operated by the staff, which patrols the jobs and enforces the union code.

Size of the Work Group and "Massification" of the Union Members:

Communication within the work group and between different groups is fragmentary and discontinuous in these jurisdictions, due to the nature of the work and the weak interaction typical in the union hall. Such weakness in both work group and the union as an independent association in the hall prevents effective informal organization and solidarity among the members. This allows for a typically low degree of exposure of staff to the rank and files. In these locals the member as an isolated individual faces the well-organized leadership group and its cadre. The rank and file's condition is that of "masses" and there is little chance for an organizational middle class.

The power of the staff is further augmented by the secondary boycott, when one local aids another in strike action by refusing to cross its picket line. If such vital functions as transportation can be stopped by agreement between leaders of different unions, the leader of the union being aided has a source of power independent of his own membership. The weaker the local is without such aid, the more crucial that leader's formal and informal relations with other union leaders will be. At the same time, the more he can depend upon such allies outside his local, the less will he have to depend upon the active support of his own members.

An extreme example may clarify the implications of this set of propositions. If a number of locals in other internationals are dependent upon one local (Teamsters, Longshoremen, or others) for their effective strike power, and if the members of the powerful union are disfranchised and have no control over their own officers, the opposition of the members may have no effect upon any of the leaders involved. It is thus possible for a leader to punish his own members by using the power of another local to close the shop down. The power of the unions in such cases is a naked pressure on the employer and the consent of the members is hardly an intervening variable. The employer, in turn, may be forced to discipline the worker for the union (22).

It must be emphasized that these are not inevitable results of either (1) the type of work group in a jurisdiction or (2) the union staff--union member relations that emerge in such work groups. However, these factors are constant due to the technological basis of work and the customary organizational strategies of these locals. They tend to shift the character of the unions away from the solidary, protest organization toward the service organization. The service organization, in turn, begins to produce the role system encountered in public and quasi-public organizations, with the union elite becoming identified in their own minds with the managerial elites. This has become formally endorsed by the leaders in certain unions; witness the "Junior partners in industry" slogan.

As the paid staff is freed from the pressure of the members, the individual participation of the rank and file and the responsibility of leaders to them approach the relation of a citizen to his governmental bureaucracy, validated on occasion by plebiscite.

LOCALS ORGANIZING LARGE, STABLE WORK GROUPS

These locals face quite different problems. Not only does the size of the plant give the average employer a greater strength relative to that of the local, but each plant is of greater importance to the union's total membership figures and total dues income. The methods of organizing are also necessarily different, with resulting differences in the staff-member relations and the basis of the staff's political power.

The Economics of Organization:

The members work together in the same place, under the same division of labor, for long periods of time. This allows the emergence of informal groups which then exercise considerable power over the individual workers. Roethlisberger and Dickson and other investigators have demonstrated in detail the effects of such groups (30). They are useful both to management and the union, in their parallel but conflicting strategies of mobilizing the workers. The union's use of such informal bonds is illustrated by this incident.

> "Our contracts say that anyone causing disharmony and fighting is discharged. So naturally, our stewards will

call a guy up if he doesn't want to join... or a couple of guys will playfully rush him up to the steward, one on each side, saying "Come on Joe, sign this bad boy up!" Naturally, he doesn't put up much resistance."

Management's manipulation of such informal groups is shown in the following remarks by an official in a CIO local.

"Sure they discriminate against minority guys. They avoid giving them job promotion. They use the race feelings of the work crews, keeping it quiet when a Negro has seniority for upgrading.
"Either they ignore his seniority, or, if he makes a noise, they tell him, 'We don't think it would work out for you to be a lead man over guys who don't like you.' Then they approach the workers and say, 'You guys wouldn't really want a nigger over you would you?' Naturally, this can work very well if the work group is not pretty idealistic-- which it usually isn't."

In these locals' plants are found the most aggressive campaigns of management to influence worker behavior, as well as the most consistent efforts of the union to gain the active participation of their members; there is little opportunity for such locals to organize from the top down. Officers of the locals are very conscious of their participation rates.

"One reason for our low participation is the bitterness of the membership over the strike and also the number of strikebreakers there are in the plants. Then there's the fraternalization policy of the big outfits. Free sports, hobby clubs, shows and so on. They make it tough for us. How many orchestras and big name comedians can we hire, to tour the country for the purpose of getting our local members out? And it's all tax free!"

It should be added that this same local has a vigorous educational program and a women's auxiliary that is very active; the local staff participates in municipal activities and gives its own dances and picnics which hundreds attend. Such locals, locked in conflict with an aggressive management, frequently justify lost strikes on the grounds that they activate the members and increase the number of the actives. (This would be sufficient ground for condemning strikes in other locals).

"That big fight wasn't very successful in terms of contract but the interest it awakened in the members, as well as the new leaders it provided, was very heartening. We got the head of our educational program out of that strike.

"The company thinks we're weaker than we are; they figure if they've got to have a union we'll be OK. They don't know that we are growing stronger all the time."

The last sentence emphasizes the stable framework for struggle between company and union in these large work forces. However, while there was little danger of the union's losing out altogether to a "no union" vote, there was another threat. If, as was usually the case, the plant was a bargaining unit, the local could be forced to protect its jurisdiction from other, raiding internationals. The officers of the local and the international representatives had to be continuously on guard to see that no rival clique in the union had gone over to another union, and to apprehend strange individuals passing around cards for representation elections. Sometimes nothing could be done to prevent the propaganda, according to one lively account.

"But, getting back to CIO, we fooled 'em once. We'd been working on the Southwestern plant for a long time, had lots of men there, and they had been pulling all their Reps down to counteract us. Well, we figured they were sucked in good, so we goes to the bridge below the plant and parks our cars, when a shift is coming off, then we run like hell to Northwestern instead. We get the little copies of our contracts out, we get the cards out, and those boys were signing as fast as they could write. Hell, they were begging for pencils. Just then someone give the tip to the CIO Reps and here they come running.

"Well sir, it's the god damnedest thing. They said, 'What the hell have you been doing with those cards? You don't want none of that baloney!' And those boys tore 'em up to a man. I just don't know what happened."

Even allowing for the informant's probable exaggeration of his success with the members of the CIO union, it is likely that the vigilance of the CIO international representatives was sensible in this case.

Status and Power of the Leaders:

The organization of large, stable work forces ordinarily precludes the hiring hall system, with its resulting control over the labor supply of management and the jobs of the members, and the policeman BA is less important. The problems of surveillance are simpler and, at the same time, the steward system becomes more effective; the local is able to use the plant's work structure as the basis for its own system of control. Stewards are chosen by department, just as the foremen are, and are frequently key men in the work. The plant work group as a whole, organized as a semi-autonomous unit, elects its grievance committee, which is the recipient of complaints, rather than the paid staff.

Stewards and committeemen are seldom full time employees of the local (none were in this sample) and they share the common job situation. Needless to say, they are exposed to the rank and file in a way that the business agent seldom is exposed -- and they are also exposed to management in a way the staff is not. This dependence of the steward on his job, and thus management, is frequently used as an argument against the steward system by craft union leaders.

> "A man working for a company is in a bad position to raise hell because then it'll put him on the hook. They'll get him, for some trivial reason, sooner or later. People exercise priveleges that are not quite kosher you know-- but they can always be caught. A steward who's given trouble on a picket line can be fired for drinking coffee-- now how the hell you gonna prove he was fired for being a steward?"

A local officer in a craft-type local summed up his opinions.

> "We've had poor experience with stewards. He over-exercises his authority; he's not trained properly--and we can't train them properly. We spend more time policing our stewards than the contract, where we have them. Now the CIO, with their weak organization, have stewards because their dues structure is too low to have personnel enough to collect dues in those open shop conditions."

Despite the eloquence of this attack on steward systems, it should be remembered that the work group is a much weaker base for a steward system in this officer's local than it is in, say, the big steel plants. In the latter, the steward is not only a representative of the local-- he is an informal leader in the plant and developes lines of power and influence within the management hierarchy as well, as Dalton has shown very clearly (8). However, he does tend to develop and use power delegated to him; this is one of the complaints of the BA quoted above. As will be shown later, this has important implications for the location of power in the local.

The counterpart of the BA in locals which have large work

groups as their jurisdiction is the international representative. This officer functions as a liaison between the plant unit and the "local-wide" organization and between both these and the international hierarchy. His function can be described as that of keeping the local in line, but it is also that of keeping the international informed. He mediates between two organized groups, on the local level, each with a basis of power.

The paid staff in the amalgamated locals, those which include several plants, are elected by the membership or by the executive board which is so elected, in contrast to the international representatives, who are "handed down from on high." These local officers (BA's, business managers or secretary-treasurers) are exposed to the membership at large chiefly during elections but they are continually dependent upon the stewards and the actives for communication and informal control in the various plant units and on the "localwide" executive board.

Thus the relative importance of the steward system in craft and industrial locals is related to the difference in the work group. Further evidence is the relative size of the steward corps. The average rate for stewards in all craft-type locals is only half that for the industrial locals. While the stewards are more plentiful and more important in the control of the industrial locals, the status and power of the professional staff leader is much weaker relative to that of the rank and filer. The ordinary member is hired by the company, not the union; union and employer contend for influence over his on-the-job behavior, as well as for his organizational loyalty in elections and negotiations.

Exposure of the Officers to the Members:

In answer to the problems posed by a stable management hierarchy and a management scheme of organization and control, the industrial local is compelled to use the plant structure for its own hierarchy of control, which runs from the informal influence of key men through steward, plant committeemen and executive board members to the "localwide" staff and the International Union. The local must gain jurisdiction and keep it by a vote of the members; it must be able to strike when the chips are down; it must be able to prevent a break in the ranks when back to work movements are started by management. At each of these points the industrial union as an organization is exposed to the rank and file of the membership.

Thus, in two modal types of work force the nature of the job conditions the types of union likely to succeed. The unions then define themselves pre-eminently as service organizations or as solidary organizations in response to the resulting organ-

<u>izational necessities; they are, in turn, so defined by their members.</u>

CONTROL AND CONSENT IN THE LOCALS:TWO REBELLIONS

To return to the question of political structure in the locals, the following hypothesis may be advanced: the organizational middle class, not irrevocably committed to the staff and sufficiently active to have influence, will generate power in locals where it is necessary to have the consent of the membership as a whole if the organization is to survive. This is apt to be true of large, stable work forces. Here the local is most vulnerable to competing elites and here rank and file participation is decisive in elections and strikes. This is less true in most unions organizing small, scattered work groups.

As a corollary to this hypothesis: the importance of the organizational middle class will increase, as the situation forces the staff to actively engage the membership in union action. The necessity to engage members is a result of crisis events, such as organizing drives, jurisdictional elections and strikes. These may be temporary or chronic, but in the industrial locals they are more apt to be ever-present possibilities. To the degree that this is true the leaders will espouse a consistent policy of engaging the membership. On the other hand, in unions with few crises, where jurisdiction is safe and management cooperative, there will be little need for such activation. In the building trades unions there are no cases of jurisdictional elections of any importance; there are no rival unions for the same membership. In these locals there is little fear of employer efforts to destroy the union.

In locals where the paid staff can safely ignore the consent of the members, even crisis situations will provoke little effort to engage them in union action. In fact, the staff may be more concerned with suppressing such activity, since it may be seen as a threat to their own control of the local. In these locals the staff depends on international support for its tenure of office, secondary boycott or management aid for control, and membership activity is simply a necessary evil.

To illustrate these propositions, brief summaries of two rebellions against local leadership, which occurred during the course of the study, will be presented. Local "A" is a large, strategically placed work force, made up of many small work groups. The average size of these groups is less than a dozen men. Local "B" is one of three competing locals in an important industry; it is a vigorous local with strong organization. An industrial local, its work groups average over five times the size of those in Local "A," and many shops have several hundred members.

Rebellion in a Craft-type Local:

Local "A" has had little local autonomy for years. It once had a policy committee, which was elected by the members to aid the international's appointee, who ruled the local. This international representative justified the lack of democratic processes in the local this way:

> "Well, they used to have elections and what a mess they got into. We had two factions that split the offices between them; they would spend all year campaigning, letting the local's business go to hell. And they didn't police the contracts-- that was the reason for putting it into trusteeship. And I can tell you it's been a lot better since they did that. It's better not to have elections when you have permanent factions that are out for personal profit and raise hell at all the meetings and are always trying to increase their power at the expense of the other side."

The utility of the "policy committee" was described in the following manner.

> "I was sent in here by the international's representative for this district as the manager. I appointed the officers and then had this policy committee elected. You know -- you need them to bring ideas and things to the rank and file. They can talk things over and talk them up. A policy committee like that was a good thing because here I'd been in six months and the members didn't know me. I was busy up here, in the union offices, and they wondered... but the policy committee helped there."

When this local went into contract negotiations, the results did not satisfy all the members. Other strong unions locally were getting a ten per cent across the board raise, in conformity with the Wage Stabilization Board's ceiling at that time. However, in the words of one rank and file active member of this local:

> "The union pulled a sell-out deal with the employers. They could have got a big raise-- everyone else was getting it-- but they signed for <u>nothing.</u> A security clause, worth about four dollars per member to the organization but nothing for the members to take home. And they pulled some fine tricks in getting it voted in.

The men have to vote, for a settlement, you know."

Or, in the words of another member:

"Nobody wanted the damned thing. But the officers had made a deal, so we voted on it. You know what? The guys that play with the officers, a handfull, had big stacks of ballots to vote with. The rest of us, damned near everybody, got only one vote apiece-- we "accepted" the contract. It was a damned steal. But you don't have any rights in our local. If you speak up you lose your job, because the local has so much power over the employers. I know of one recent case like that."

The situation was further complicated, however, by the entrance of a "paper" organization, regarded as a professional union-breaking group by the leaders in Los Angeles unions. This organization, whose income derives directly from management, has tactics which are described by leaders who have fought it as "literally enforcing Taft-Hartley, which is all it takes to hurt us."

As the rank and file of Local A was already stirred up over the contract issue, the paper organization chose it as a target for a disorganization campaign. According to the business manager of the local it went like this.

"This character comes and starts a rank and file rump against me. He plants a guy in the union and gets a few others together and they raise hell. He has such a bad reputation, though, that it's easy to show them what is really up. I used the La Follette Reports for instance. In fact, that move was good for me. The boys didn't know what the union was until they see us fighting some outfit like that. Then they get worried and more involved and interested in keeping their union."

When the manager was asked if there were any dissidents on his policy committee, he replied as follows.

"Well, yes, one was interested in his ideas, but he got fired out of the industry and later on he decided that he'd been wrong. But he couldn't keep his committee job after he got fired, you see. We have a rule like that. Well, after this deal blew over, the International sent me instructions to abolish the policy committee and appointed me an Executive Council. So what I did was appoint my Council out of the elected members of the old policy committee."

(The italicized statements should be compared with the remarks of the member quoted earlier. They indicate an important mechanism of control in such a local.)

According to another active member:

"There was lots of resentment against that contract. The men knew they were being sold out and run for the benefit of a small, tightly-knit clique. But that raid must have been a God-send. I saw some of the literature they aimed at the rank and file, and it was pretty awful. 'The Taft-Hartley Law is for the benefit of the union member,' for example."

In this local at present the only vestige of local autonomy is the Executive Council, hand-picked by the manager, who is himself responsible only to the international hierarchy. There is no organized resistance to this state of affairs and another rebellion would have as little chance as the one described above. That this state of affairs is not unusual in a few internationals is evidenced by the remarks of a labor leader when the story was repeated to him. "They're disappointed because the election was rigged? Good God, they're lucky to have a chance to vote at all, much less a chance to *win*!"

Rebellion in an Industrial Local:

Local "B" was controlled by a strong Communist Party fraction from the time it entered CIO. It was organized from the first by plant units with a chief steward in each plant, but the "localwide" officers were chosen through elections by the members at large, held in the union hall.

The local was largely ethnic, with a preponderant group of Mexicans. The Negroes voted consistently as a cadre for the staff members. Since, however, many plant units were predominantly Mexican and since Mexicans had always been an important part of the labor force in the industry, two-thirds of the chief stewards were Mexican.

One of these Mexican chief stewards at an important plant, who will be called Marquez, had developed considerable influence with the Mexican membership. This had been encouraged by the local's leaders, undoubtedly as a coopting device. Though not a party member, he was undoubtedly trusted by the cadre. The local's leadership group was uneasy about the Mexicans, since their own strategy was, in general, to emphasize the Negro member's welfare. As a Mexican active remarked, "*You see, they don't much like Mexicans because Mexicans are Catholic.*" There were undoubtedly other reasons for reliance upon the Negroes. For one thing, they were concentrated in a few plants and highly manipulable as a cadre, while Mexicans were more difficult to control and less useful, being scattered in the plants and having poor attendance at the routine meetings.

Marquez was a member of the executive board of the local for years and a member of the local's negotiating committee consistently. His function as a spokesman for the Mexicans yielded him a considerable personal influence.

Then, in the postwar political climate, the increasing manipulation of the local by the Communist leadership began to lose members and hurt the organizing activity. The decline was due to a number of specific causes; one was the use of the "communist issue" against the union by employers and other locals, and another was the use of the local's funds for non-union purposes. There were other unpleasant handicaps, but all may be summed up by one general statement: the demands of the Communist Party upon the fraction which controlled the local ran directly counter to the demands of the local as a trade union.

In early 1950 the Communist and Communist-sympathetic staff decided to disaffiliate the local from its CIO international, to which it had belonged for over ten years-- probably because this international was being purged and was removing Communist identified officers from the organization. When this move was brought before the members, however, there was considerable resistance, especially among the Mexican members. led by Marquez. The local's executive board then deposed him as chief steward, but the shop committee at his plant upheld him. The committee was then dissolved by the executive board, and another elected. The membership in the plant, however, reelected the entire slate, including Marquez. He remained *de facto* leader of the Mexican faction in the local.

According to Marquez:

> "The big rift came with disaffiliation. We challenged them for a referendum and a secret ballot on the issue of getting out of CIO-- and they refused because they knew they'd get beaten and be out automatically. We knew then we'd be able to turn the trick (i.e., set up a new local and capture the membership, S.G.). The international president was cautious though-- he didn't think we could do it. I told him, 'Either we'll do it with your help or we'll do it anyway.' Then he came along."

Since the hall-centered local organization was controlled by the old cadre, the breakaway local was set up as a separate union and, in the Fall of 1949, began to raid the old local plant by plant. This was made easier by the plant unit organizations, many of which were headed by Mexican stewards. The following conversation between Marquez and three of his rank and file organizers gives some notion of the tactics used.

> Marquez: "Yeah, it's working all right. Always from within, playing their game and meantime working on our own set-up."
> Organizer: "Before you go any further, there's one thing I want to bring up. I wanted an apron the other day, when I was on the machine. It says in our contract we get supplied with them when we need them. So I went to the chief steward and I told him: 'It says we get 'em and I want one.' Well, you know he looked at me and said, 'You can't have it; I can't get it.' I said, 'What the hell?' 'Why,' says he, 'that contract is no good. We can't enforce it.' "
> Marquez: "Is that right? (makes a note) Well, that looks pretty good. You and I know what's going on there. They got three different kinds of union guys in that shop; the old gang, our fellows, and the company union the boss is promoting... By the way, you boys count them cards like I asked you? (e.g., the cards at the time clock in the plant, giving breakdowns of workers by department, S.G.)
> The results are tallied by department.
> Marquez: "Well, did you see anyone you knew in Shipping?"
> Organizer: "Four of our boys in there. We are gonna take the Shipping department easy."
> Marquez: "Well, I wouldn't try to use more than one good man. No use letting the cat out of the bag. Who's good?"
> Organizer: "Martinez. There's a good boy. And his brother, Jack is foreman-- they're very close. He ought to be just the boy. We could give him a little expense money."
> Marquez: (nodding) "Well, I tell you-- the thing he better do is make house-to-house calls on every man in Shipping. You go with him. That's the best way."

In this manner the campaign progressed; from the charter group of a few hundred in 1950 the breakaway local reached 700 by December and nearly 2,000 by the following summer. The issues used in the campaign appear in the following statement, made by Marquez, to the organizers.

"The Communist issue splits them and breaks the ice.

> But that's not enough. The old local gets good contracts too. That won't do. It's his deals that gets him in trouble and makes our ammunition. He negotiated those contracts in September giving the guys five or ten cents an hour, then he made personal deals allowing them to speed up; that way it didn't cost the employers nothing. But the war in Korea helps a lot and the local is broke. It's contributed money to every front outfit in the country. Tell the members, 'You paid your dues, and when you go on strike, what's in the treasury?' They know what it means."

Thus the new leadership tended to mute the communist issue (indicating something of the kind of hold Communist leaders have in such locals).

> "The main thing you gotta remember is that those guys were good leaders. They'd fight and die for the union-- you could never say they wouldn't fight for their members, because they damned well would. The secretary's a Communist and he'd give up his house, his car, his family, for the job he had to do. His job was union because that was part of their political program. He didn't care that much about the union, but he cared about his job as a party member. Looky what he done for the party-- taken a cut from $150.00 a week to $65.00 a week and he'd take more. When he came to town he didn't even have a pair of good shoes; now he has a $15,000.00 home and drives a good car. But he'd give it all up. No sir, you can't say he's not a fine leader. He's good as they come and he knows all the tricks of the trade.
>
> "The main thing that's caused us to break off is not that he's a communist. Hell, he could go out after hours and preach communism and work for it and we wouldn't care. That's nothing to us so long as he does his union job. But he can't use union time and union money and the union's name. How many times do you see in the *People's World*, "The Membership of Local *** Is Solidly Behind-" something or other, when the membership is no such thing. Hell, our membership is anti-communist and always has been. But they're liberal and believe in progressive things, so don't make a mistake when they talk back and call them communists."

Such considerations limited, severely, the kinds of issues that could be used.

"No, the one thing we've got to say over and over, because it's the truth and because we're dealing with members who are union men and who know the truth is this: they have put a political program before the interests of our local. They have marked the local and everybody knows it. They have made quick contracts and beg for little raises from the bosses, because the bosses know they're Communist and out of CIO. Everybody knows they have no backing and it's killing the local as a union. They've lost membership, lost elections, lost strikes, can't enforce contracts--all because of that political affiliation. They're good leaders but a leader is nothing unless he's got power behind him. They haven't got it and won't get it."

These issues were taken to the workers in plant after plant, through key men friendly to the breakaway group, frequently through the stewards of the old union who were friendly to Marquez. The new local won election after election. In these representation elections the unions competing often numbered as many as four. The workers had to be persuaded to come in and to do this key men had to be activated. The new local was possible only because of informal organizing among the workers in the plants-- through informal groups in the various departments.

Job Structure and Power Structure; Implications of the Rebellions:

A basic difference between these two locals in states of crisis is the degree of dependence of the staff leaders upon the membership as a whole. The much greater vulnerability of the leaders in Local "B" is due to the union's associational base in large plant forces and the development of centers of strength at the plant level. The leaders of Local "B" attempted to solve this through making the chief stewards in the plants responsible for control, while keeping the policy-making decisions for the "localwide" organization, which could be manipulated by the cadre.

The results are significant. If, to use Selznick's statement, "delegation is the primal act of organization," then it may be said that the officers of Local "B" were forced to extend delegation to centers far beyond their control (35). In the new breakaway local the relevant formal structure was designed to take this into account. The labor movement, like all organizational forms in our society, is necessarily engaged in experiments (though to the leaders involved it may appear, as Perleman has remarked, a matter of "desperate expediency");

the results of the experiment in Local "B" are reported by Marquez.

> "You never see voting by minority basis, by race or color, now. People vote by shops-- that's why I got them to elect the executive board on a shop basis. The board is controlled easier if it's elected by the union as a whole. It's too damned easy to get your officers forming cliques with the executive board. The way it is now in our local, the paid officers *can't* control the board members-- they're independent as hell when they come up here for a meeting. But you know, the members fought it when I suggested this kind of a board to them.
> "I said to them: ' Look, you got rid of the Communists-- doesn't it occur to you that I can do the same things to you that they did?' Now that they've got this system they like it."

Such a formal structure in a local has the effect of giving both responsibility and power to officers elected from the plant units. The stewards are responsible as before but now have representation at the seat of "localwide power," the executive board. The result is to increase the pressure of the membership on the staff but, at the same time, to increase communication between staff and members. The structure should prevent the recurrence of the crisis which brought it about.

The statement of Marquez contrasts sharply with a summary statement made by the business manager of Local "A" with respect to democracy in the unions.

> "The locals with autonomous status tend to just stand still or else to lose ground. You take *them;* now you can judge if the officers are doing a job by how the organizing is going. You can see if they're following the lines of least resistance, just drawing a check every week and taking it easy and keeping the political situation favorable to them.
> "I tell you, you have a popularity contest for your democracy and democracy can be a mighty dangerous thing for your organization if that's what you've got. The boy who comes in on a popularity contest has got to keep that popularity, at the cost of the local organization.
> "In fact, the trusteeship method is best. Our history shows that the progress of the International has depended on the *locals in receivership* (i.e., those whose members cannot elect officers, S.G.)."

Rather than taking a defensive stand, the manager of the disfranchised Local "A" praised his union's political system on theoretical and moral grounds."The locals without autonomy are the ones that organize the unorganized and get wages and working conditions for them." His statement is that of Marquez in reverse. His emphasis is upon the loss of freedom for the staff when there is a more democratic framework of control. The two positions are possible alternatives with respect to a fundamental dilemma in the unions, one which goes as deep as the strength of the several functions which union organizations serve in the social system. If the union is seen primarily as an administrative and regulative organization, the leader of Local "A" is correct; (popularity contests interfere with the organizing). If it is seen as primarily a solidary, protest movement, the leader of Local "B" is correct: the members must have a visible structure for expressing consent, enthusiasm or censure.

In Local "A" the leaders are dealing with an extreme case of a union based upon small, fluid, work groups. The membership is classed as low in socio-economic status, with no job differentiation. Members are widely scattered in places of work and move frequently from job to job. Few of the work groups escape that close personal relation with supervision known as foreman domination, for they usually work in groups of a half dozen or so men, closely watched by foremen. There is little basis for a strong social group at the work place.

The membership of Local "B" is occupationally highly differentiated, with jobs running from unskilled labor to highly skilled and well paid jobs as craftsmen. It is highly concentrated, with half the members working in six large plants; these are too large to encourage foreman domination and large enough to allow effective strike power on the part of a plant unit. Associated with this is the possibility of effective plant-unit organization. The large plant unit can manage many of its own affairs and is too large to be easily controlled by a roving business agent. The "localwide" leadership cannot afford to ignore these plant unit organizations as long as they have a degree of freedom to choose, for they can effectively "strike" their own locals.

The basis for the existence of a strong organizational middle class in the locals of this sample emerges from comparing these two locals. The crucial factor is the existence, or non-existence, of organized, self-conscious units at the work group level. If the union exists for the rank and file member at the job level, then, at this level he can and will participate in the functioning of the organization. And he will affect the leadership group by his action.

CHAPTER VI

POLITICAL STRUCTURE AND ETHNIC REPRESENTATION

Craft-type unions, based on small, fluid work groups, generally have "localwide" officers whose election and policy are independent of any organized group at a lower level. In these locals control is through a cadre created by the leadership, which manipulates meetings and elections. The staff captures the local union organization. Frequently, however, the international hierarchy captures the staff and controls it through appointment.

Industrial locals, based on large, stable work groups, are not as vulnerable to international capture; however, cadre control is possible. While the nature of the work group makes it possible for the local to develop reciprocal control processes between members and leaders, it does not make such a development inevitable. Certain locals have effective plant-unit organizations, but others have a local union which, as a social group, is based solely upon interaction during the occasional meetings of the members in the union hall.

If the hypothesis, that the organizational middle-class is the key structural prerequisite for reciprocal control, is useful, such control should be more likely in the locals with plant-unit organizations, and two-way influence should be the net product. Executive boards of the locals with plant-unit organization should be more directly representative of the members and less a result of "your officers forming cliques with the executive board." The rank order of representation should follow this pattern:

Most representation: industrial locals with plant-units
Less representation: industrial locals without plant-units

HALL-ORIENTED LOCALS AND PLANT-ORIENTED LOCALS

The industrial locals may be divided clearly into two types; the two differ basically in the degree of integration between the work group and the formal union structure. Where there is close integration between the two, the locals will be called "Plant-oriented," for here the union identifies itself organizationally with the place of work. Where the two are separated with little overlap in groups or representatives, the local will be called "Hall-oriented"; in these locals the union is primarily an organization centered on the union hall.

Plant-oriented Locals:

These have strong plant units, organized on a semi-autonomous basis. The control of the rank and file over the stewards is extended to control of the executive board, for it is elected by the plant constituency. Thus the organization of the members at the work place is directly channelled into the "localwide" organization. This forms the basis for an organizational middle class in the local, committed to the plant constituencies as well as the leadership of the local. The local's middle-class, with access to power, acts as a limit on the action of the staff and a source of possible competition; from these executive boards new leaders arise. In such locals international support and control are less mandatory and less possible; indeed, they provide a base for the possible control of the international by the local unions.

Hall-oriented Locals:

In these unions the plant is not organized as a separate unit. The steward has little influence upon the "localwide" leadership and becomes, in fact, its instrument. The "localwide" organization of the union is not related, structurally, to the members' on-the-job associations, and the executive board as well as the top leaders are elected in mass meetings held in the union hall. Such leadership is apt to be the product of mass manipulation and the action of organizational cadres. The cadres then allow the officers the freedom from the rank and file common to craft-type locals; however, they do have to "work at it" more. Elections do occur, members do associate in the plants, and therefore the stewards with their plant followings may be necessary to the cadre. This does not occur in any predictable fashion, however; the stewards are, themselves, components of a "massified" lower leadership.

The chain of influence and power originating in the lower levels of the union structure may be seen from the leader's point of view as a chain of dependence. Leaders of the craft locals are dependent on their international, leaders of the Hall-oriented locals, on their cadres; leaders in the Plant-oriented locals are dependent upon the organizational middle-class of their union, localized in the various plants, but organized through the "localwide" system of referenda and, more important, the local's executive board.

A Comparison of the Two Types of Locals:

Six of the industrial locals in this sample are Hall-oriented, and seven are Plant oriented. One of the Hall-oriented locals was CIO, one was ex-CIO, four were AFL in their affiliations. One Plant-oriented local was AFL, one was ex-CIO and four were AFL affiliates. Although the Plant-oriented local was more common in CIO, the classification cut across federation lines. Furthermore, CIO locals in the Hall-oriented class were more like other Hall-oriented locals than they were like any local in the Plant-oriented group: the same was true for the AFL local in the latter category.

Size of the Work Group and Role of the Steward:

The average shop size of the plants is closely related to the type of political control, as would be expected from the above discussion. The following table is based upon crude averages, but the wide differences lend these significance.

TABLE 6-1

MEAN SIZE OF PLANT IN THREE TYPES OF LOCALS

TYPE OF LOCAL UNION	Average No. of Men Working Together				
	0 - 19	20 - 39	40 - 59	60 - 79	80 +
Craft	7	1			
Hall-Oriented	1	2	3		
Plant-Oriented			1	3	3

Plant-oriented locals commonly organize large groups of workers, Hall-oriented locals, smaller groups, and in the craft-type local the work groups ordinarily do not average over a dozen. Steward systems based on these work groups increase in strength with the size of the work group. In craft-type locals three unions have no steward system, one large local has none for two-thirds of its members and stewards generally have neither power nor status. A leader in a craft-type local discusses his stewards.

> "Now we've got stewards at some of our plants. Two of them are colored boys, and they do alright. They weren't elected, they were hand-picked. We always pick our stewards. They were picked because of their

> interest in the organization and because they won't stick their necks out too far. They have specific jobs. (Question: What kind of jobs?)
> "They notify us when a non-union man is hired and then when we have a dismissal come up, we always discuss it before hand. The BA, the personnel manager, the guy getting fired and the steward, all meet and discuss it. The steward tells the BA what he thinks and we thrash it out."

Stewards are, for the most part, a handy adjunct to the BA in craft-type locals. The position is no basis for political influence. In all industrial locals, however, a real effort is made to use the steward system, for reasons noted earlier. Both Plant-oriented and Hall-oriented locals average a steward for each twenty-five members; because of the larger plants in the Plant-oriented locals, however, their stewards would usually be members of a corps, rather than isolated.

Plant-unit Association:

The Plant-oriented locals are the only ones in the sample which have regularly scheduled meetings of the plant units. In these meetings the union as an on-the-job reality for the members is directly joined to the local as a separate organizational entity. Hall-oriented locals have such meetings only in crisis situations and craft-type locals usually do not have them at all. Plant-oriented locals also elect committees, frequently by plant: Hall-oriented locals have committees appointed by "localwide" officers, while the craft-type unions ordinarily do not have committees.

In Plant-oriented locals the area of membership participation includes both meetings in the shop and meetings in the union hall; the local is adapted to the job-oriented unionism of the rank and file members. The formal structure, as noted earlier, allows greater ease of participation, shortening the physical and social distance between member and union. Since attendance at the plant-unit meetings is ordinarily high, the structure allows a continuity of organization and communication which strengthens the union in the plants and, at the same time, strengthens the plant-unit in the localwide organizational control system.

Participation in Localwide Activity:

There is considerable evidence that plant-unit organization strengthens participation in the "localwide" organization. The usual attendance at General Membership meetings averages eighteen per cent in the Plant-oriented locals, as against eight per cent in the Hall-oriented locals. And, since the percentage voting in Special Election meetings is almost identical, the percentage increase in attendance at elections is much higher in the Hall-oriented locals. It has been suggested that such an increase measures the proportion of uninformed, manipulable, voters. To read this relationship in another way, if those who come to General Membership meetings also come to Special Election meetings (which is plausible in view of the greater interest the latter have for all members) then of those members who vote in the Plant-oriented locals almost half are individuals who also attend the routine meetings of the local. Of the voters in the Hall-oriented locals, less than one-fifth also attend the General Membership meetings. If the above reasoning is correct, the Plant-oriented locals' member should be less susceptible to distortion and manipulation of issues.

This analysis is hampered with respect to the craft-type locals by the scarcity of data. Of the eight locals in this category, two are under receivership and have no elections, two have not had an election in over three years, and one local has a heavy fine for failure to attend any meeting. (The absence of data is important in itself). It is not reasonable to compare the three remaining locals with the two groups described.

POLITICAL SYSTEM AND ETHNIC REPRESENTATION

If this distinction between Plant-oriented and Hall-oriented locals is useful, it should make a difference in the Mexican and Negro representation in the leadership structure. For, if the Plant-oriented structure allows more participation by actives while control by cadres becomes more difficult, such participation should give the Mexicans and Negroes a chance to become leaders at the same time that their interests become live issues. Although a completely equalitarian ethnic situation would be one in which the relationship between ethnic membership and ethnic proportion of the board would be about proportional with random variation, this is unlikely to occur where ethnic discrimination exists. Instead, the ethnic issue should result in equal or above equal representation for Mexicans and Negroes in leadership positions.

The representation of Mexicans and Negroes in the leadership hierarchy of the locals compared with their proportion in the membership is given in Table VI, Appendix "A". Data for executive board representation are summarized in the following table. The representation rate is computed by dividing the proportion of members in an ethnic contingent into the proportion of offices held by these ethnic contingents. If representation is similar to that for the total members it should average 1.00.

TABLE 6-2

Executive Board Representation Rates for Ethnic* Contingents in Two Types of Industrial Local

RANGE OF RATES	TOTAL Plant/	Hall	MEXICANS Plant/	Hall	NEGROES Plant/	Hall
.00	---	5	---	2	---	3
.01 - .50	2	4	1	3	1	1
.51 - 1.00	5	2	3	1	2	1
1.00 - 1.50	3	---	2	---	1	---
Over 1.50	2	---	1	---	1	---
	12	11	7	6	5	5

* Contingents amounting to less than ten per cent of the total members are omitted.

The difference is striking and supports the hypothesis, despite the size of the sample. Of twenty-three contingents, one-fourth are unrepresented; all are in Hall-oriented locals. Of five contingents over-represented, all are in Plant-oriented locals. Eighty per cent of the Plant-oriented local contingents are represented at above one-half proportional; almost ninety per cent in the Hall-oriented locals are represented at less than half proportional.

The mean and the range of representation rates for each type of local strengthen the conclusion. The mean for Plant-oriented locals is 1.02 for Mexican contingents, with a range from .47 to 2.08; it is 1.02 for Negro contingents also, with a range from .45 to 1.83. In the Hall-oriented locals, in contrast, the mean for Mexican contingents is .29 and the range is from zero (no representation) to .72; the mean for Negroes is .23 with a range from zero to .74. The representation of Mexicans and Negroes is consistently higher in the Plant-oriented locals.

Representation vs. Cooptation:

The possibility remains that these executive board members are coopted; that they merely represent "fronts" for the real rulers of the locals. There is no way of knowing for certain if this is the case, on the basis of these data, but the test used with ethnic staff members may be applied and the board analyzed according to the absolute numbers of Mexicans and Negroes on the board. It is plausible to expect that "guys to represent the minority groups," as they are known in the more autocratic locals, would not be chosen in large numbers, since they would then present the threat of a voting bloc on the board which might generate power and create embarassing problems for the staff. The number of ethnic board members in the locals is given in the following table; the mean number of ethnic board members in craft-type unions is indicated for comparison.

TABLE 6-3

The Mean Number of Ethnic Board Members in Three Types of Local Union

MEAN NO. OF BOARD MEMBERS	PLANT-ORIENTED	HALL-ORIENTED	CRAFT-TYPE
Mexican	7.4	2.0	1.4
Negro	3.7	1.0	1.6
Total Ethnic	11.1	3.0	3.0
(All Members)	(29)	(14)	(12)

The average size of the ethnic contingents on the boards of the Plant-oriented locals, seven for Mexicans and four for Negroes, lends support to the supposition that they are less likely to be fronts for a controlling leadership than in the Hall-oriented locals, and are more likely to constitute an effective force in the politics of the union. And, though the executive boards are larger in these locals, the proportions of ethnic members are also larger. (It should be noted that a larger board may be less amenable to staff domination in any case.)

Furthermore, there is a comparable difference in the composition of the steward corps, though not so striking as in the case of the board members. When the mean representation rates, together with the ranges, are considered, the two ethnic groups appear to be more consistently close to proportional representation in the Plant-oriented than in the Hall-oriented locals.

The definition of the steward's rank also varies with the type of local. That definition, current in the craft-type locals, is implicit in the words of the business agent quoted earlier. A test of the stewards' importance may be contrived by taking the ethnic minorities representation rate on the executive board as a fraction of its rate for stewards. If there is a close correspondence between the two rates, the fraction should be around 1.00; if it is less than this, the contingent is represented at steward but not at the executive board level.

TABLE 6-4

Representation Rate for Executive Board Members As a Proportion of the Rate for Stewards *

TYPE OF LOCAL	MEXICANS		NEGROES	
	MEAN	RANGE	MEAN	RANGE
Plant-oriented	1.26	.61 - 2.28	1.17	.38 - 2.44
Hall-oriented	.54	.00 - 2.00	1.12	.00 - 4.00

* Contingents less than ten per cent of the membership omitted.

These indexes show the distance between the on-the-job organization of the union and the "localwide" level. The closer relationship in the Plant-oriented locals conforms to what would be predicted on the basis of the hypotheses outlined earlier. The zeros indicate steward representation without executive board membership; there were four such cases in the Hall-oriented locals, none in the Plant-oriented group.

Data on staff members are not amenable to the sort of analysis that has been used with stewards and executive board members; the leadership population is so small that average rates would be misleading. However, in the Hall-oriented locals, fifty-five per cent of the members are ethnic, but only sixteen per cent of the staff are so identified; forty per cent of the Plant-oriented locals' members are ethnic and, if the locals with only regional staff are omitted (and each has an ethnic officer at this level) the staff numbers fourteen; of these four are ethnic. These data are crude but point in the direction of validating the guiding hypothesis. For, as at other levels of leadership, Mexicans and Negroes are substantially better represented in these locals. (And, if the regional staff were included, over forty per cent of the staff in the Plant-oriented unions is ethnic.)

Another Hypothesis: Job Level and Ethnic Representation:

Although this dichotomy of the locals distinguishes sharply between those in which Mexicans and Negroes are represented and not represented, consistently, at all levels of leadership, there remains the possibility that the differences are really due to other variations between the two groups of organizations. One obvious hypothesis is a difference in job-level which, coinciding with the difference in political structure, could produce the difference in ethnic representation. If more Negro members were unskilled in the Hall-oriented group, this might account for their lack of representation as leaders.

At every level of skill, the Plant-oriented contingents are better represented on the executive boards of the locals. And, when the proportion of the skilled workers made up of Negroes or Mexicans is taken as an independent variable, the same results occur; whether with a large proportion of the key men or not, contingents in the Plant-oriented locals have political office. In the Hall-oriented locals they have no office if there are no key-men; and, even if they are heavily represented in this group, they do not have their proportional share of office.

The difference in representation rates for Mexicans and Negroes between the two classes of locals cannot be explained by job-level of the ethnic workers. The Hall or Plant orientation of the local is the most useful tool for predicting and understanding the relative representation of Mexicans and Negroes in the union's political structure.

THE ANATOMY OF POWER AND THE ETHNIC TRACER

In the previous chapter the local unions were analyzed with respect to the associational base upon which the union is built and its effect upon the political system of the local. The differences in control structure possible between locals with a small fluid work group as base or with a large, stable work force were emphasized. It was noted that the large work group typically forces the leadership to engage the members to a greater extent than does the small, isolated work group. The description of two rebellions, one in a large industrial-type local and the other in a craft-type local, illustrated this point. Industrial work forces lead to organization at the job level and this in turn may give the membership effective means of influencing the top leadership.

But this is not necessarily so. There must be organizational channels from the rank and file organization at the plant level to the "localwide" leadership. This occurs only in certain locals. Thus it may be said that (1) in some industrial locals there is rank and file participation at the plant unit level, carried upward to the executive board level where influence on the staff is possible; (2) there is plant level rank and file interaction in other industrial locals but it has little effect on the "localwide" organization and the staff; (3) there is scanty rank and file participation in the craft-type locals at the job level, and not much relationship between the union as a Hall-centered organization and the job-oriented unionism of the members.

The emergence of an effective organizational middle class in the locals requires, however, (1) participation by the rank and file at the level where the union has meaning for them, that is, the plant or shop level, (2) the delegation of power to the actives at this level and (3) effective representation of these actives at the seat of "localwide" power, the executive board and officers of the local. Such an organizational middle class is rare (though not impossible) in craft-type locals. It exists, in embryo, in the Hall-oriented locals, through the informal work groups and their leaders, but it is not structurally related to the "localwide" organization. It is found as an effective political force only in the Plant-oriented locals, those which have functioning plant-unit organizations and executive boards elected from plant constituencies.

When the locals of the sample are grouped into three classes, Plant-oriented, Hall-oriented and Craft-type, there are sharp and consistent differences in the rate of Mexican and Negro representation in leadership, relative to their numbers in the locals. Plant-oriented locals have a higher and more consistent rate at all levels of leadership; so clear and consistent are the differences between them and the Hall-oriented locals that this is taken to substantiate the proposition that those officers elected in Plant-oriented locals will be most representative of the membership.

Then, if the ethnic issue be considered a special case of the interests of the members, it can be said that the Plant-oriented local is the union structure in which participation of the members on a realistic, non-manipulated level is most likely to occur and influence policy. The staff is exposed to pressure from plant units precisely because these units are social groups basic to the ongoing of the local. They have a continuity of association due to the continuity of the job; they have an immediate relevance for the members and, by the same token, are much easier for the members to participate in as a concrete social group. However, to function in this manner the plant group must have formal structure and this must be articulated with the control system of the local as a whole.

Once the members participate in Plant-units of the local, the relationship between staff and membership tends to become reciprocal, with a consequent increase of pressure on the administrative officers of the local; this forces them to gain consent and to activate the members politically. Such is undoubtedly one reason for the more consistent representation of depressed ethnic minorities in such locals: they have genuine political power. The plant units, which allow the rank and file as a whole to influence the officers, serve the Mexicans and Negroes who work in these plants in the same way. And, at the other extreme, in certain of the Craft-type locals where the rank and file are disfranchised or captive, the ethnic contingents are similarly helpless.

CHAPTER VII

WHEN RACE IS AN ISSUE IN THE LOCAL UNION

The representation of ethnic members in the control structure of a local represents at least a partial victory for the minority population; they have achieved high status roles within the organization. Whether this achievement is reflected in the general status of minority members within the local or on the job cannot, however, be deduced from representation alone. It is necessary to understand the empirical limits and possibilities of the union as an action agency.

These limits can be derived through the analysis of what happens through time with given kinds of locals combined with the analysis of what constitutes a "live issue" to the leaders. An international representative of one CIO union, an intellectual and a liberal, once commented on the contemporary union scene in Los Angeles as follows:

> "Hell, you've got no direction, no philosophy, in labor now. You used to could sit down and talk about the movement with the guys in it-- but no more. They look at you, like you were crazy, and usually tell you, 'Hell, it ain't practical!"

If ethnic issues in the local must be "live issues" to precipitate union action then they must be "practical." Such issues, changing as ideology changes, are always those which are important for the tenure of union officers, their success and failure, or the existence of their local. The proportion of the membership made up of ethnic workers does not determine the existence of a race issue, since locals with large contingents have no problems; it is the impingement of an ethnic population on the organizational structure which raises an ethnic issue.

A TYPOLOGY OF LOCALS AND ITS BEARING ON THE ISSUE

In accounting for those instances where race was found to be alive as an issue in this sample of locals, both of the earlier analyses of control in the locals are useful. The categories "craft-type," "Hall-oriented" and "plant-oriented" local, have utility in accounting for the access, or lack of it, which

Mexicans and Negroes have to the leadership positions. In another chapter, approaching the control system in terms of the leadership's source of power, three configurations of dependence were described as common to the sample. Logically, then, there are nine possible types of local leadership situations in the sample. However, the two classifications are not independent of one another; almost all of the locals studied fall in one of four classes, as the following table shows.

TABLE 7-1

POWER ORIENTATION AND EXPOSURE TO THE MEMBERSHIP: TWENTY-ONE LOCAL LEADERSHIP GROUPS

POWER ORIENTATION	EXPOSURE TO THE MEMBERSHIP Craft-Type	Hall-Oriented	Plant-Oriented
International-Dominated	3		
Captive	4		
Membership Dominated	1	6	7

Craft-type locals are almost always either International-dominated or Captive; both Plant-oriented and Hall-oriented industrial locals are in the Membership-dominated category.

The division of the Craft-type locals into International-dominated and Captive locals points back to the union fragmentation of the work force. These locals separate the workers with no intrinsic strike power from those with great strike power and in the resulting web of alliances the true craftsman's unions tend to control the one-job locals. The rarity of Membership-domination among the Craft-type locals is due to the scattered and fluid nature of the work group, and lack of membership pressures allows international domination or capture. The one Membership-dominated local in the Craft-type class was the Retail Clerks, a local which has adequate strike power without any help from other craft locals and, like industrial locals, one which organizes all of the work force in the markets and stores.

In the industrial locals, in contrast, the membership of workers at all levels in one union (1) guarantees strike power for the local and (2) requires the consent of the members which (3) results in either plant-unit organization or machine-rule from the union hall.

The ethnic status quo and the emergence of race as an issue will be described for the four types of local union which dominate this sample. These are (1) International-dominated Craft-type locals; (2) Captive Craft-type locals; (3) Hall-oriented locals which are Membership-dominated and (4) Plant-oriented locals, also Membership-dominated.

The union can affect the status of Mexicans and Negroes by encouraging participation by the rank and file in the union organization, allowing them access to the leadership ladder and representation in the decision-making process in the local. The union can also affect job opportunities for these workers, not by opening a labor force to them, but by protecting their status when they enter. Seniority rules, supervision of promotion and similar devices are important norms to consider in this respect. In the following discussion both aspects of union influence will be described for ethnic contingents in each of the four kinds of union noted above.

INTERNATIONAL-DOMINATED CRAFT LOCALS

Participation:

In these unions there is very little participation by any of the members and the Mexican and Negro contingents are less involved than the average. None of the professional staff is Negro and there is only one Mexican, in a local under receivership. Stewards are chosen for compliance and for this reason there are ethnic stewards. In another such local, the professional leader said, "Oh yes, we have Ed on the executive board -- you know, to represent the minority guys." This is an unusual luxury for minority members in locals of this type.

Job-protection:

In two of these locals there is no local autonomy and in all of them the members use the local chiefly as a service organization; the hiring hall is of great importance. Indications are that Negroes and Mexicans have very uneven chances of getting the more desirable jobs. The president of one local stated it as axiomatic that Negroes are concentrated on swing and graveyard shifts. The casual low-grade jobs are frequently night operations. The president said, however:

"There is no program here. Each member is treated equally and judged on his ability. But the least said, the better. We don't want to bring the issue up when it isn't necessary. We don't want to make the colored man feel that he is equal; this would be unfair to him and would upset the apple cart."

A member of the local, a Negro, discussed his problem.

"Sure, I'll talk to you, but don't use my name because things is tough enough the way it is. I've worked one day in the past two weeks and I've been here early every morning. I know that sometimes my name is at the top of the list but other guys is called first... But what are you gonna do? If I squawk, they'll never call my name."

Another Negro was slightly more optimistic.

"I've been out of steady work about four months. I usually get two or three days work out of here--that's with Sunday night. I'm pretty sure of that Sunday night job. Most of us colored fellows are pretty sure of picking up that Sunday night work. They always want us then. Somebody's got to work those box cars, and it might as well be us."

Negroes amounted to a large proportion of this local's membership during the wartime labor shortage. The union, however, has not protected their jobs. Their presence was, in the words of the BA, due to the fact that the companies had "to scrape the bottom of the barrel during the war." He said there is now an extensive effort on the part of the industry to "clean out" the Negroes, and he named a number of major firms whose large Negro crews had practically all been let go.

Representation:

This local, with large numbers of Negroes and Mexicans among its members, has no ethnic representation in the leadership. Its constitution and its hiring hall rules say "There shall be no discrimination in the dispatching of members from the hall or the acceptance of members by the employer in the case." The BA remarked, however, that some companies refused to hire Negroes and there was a long standing, tacit, agreement between the union's dispatchers and the companies. This understanding is known and accepted by the local's staff.

The manager of the local explained that it was not his job as a union official to upset the status quo in race relations, that he had to concentrate on maintaining a working relationship with the industry where his union operated. He said the union, under no circumstances, would tolerate discrimination if it were practiced by one union member against another. Otherwise the union assumed that the employer has the right to specify the type of worker wanted and it is not up to the union to force unwanted personnel into a company.

From the other end, one of the chief employers of the local's membership was interviewed:

> (Question: Is any group prohibited from working here?)
> "No, -- only the colored people, of course."
> (Question: Are Negroes automatically "out" or would you hire them under some circumstances?)
> "Why, if the union would send them, we would accept them. The whole industry is unionized, you know."

This executive went on to say that personnel policy was decided locally, with wide margins for decisions. He thought that the Negroes could work just as well as anyone else. The company did employ a few men from the South, and he believed the men in general might resent having to work alongside Negroes. Customers were another matter.

> "We <u>have</u> had notices from our customers about having Negroes in our company. No, usually just a hint or a suggestion. Pleasing our customers is our first consideration. There hasn't been a Negro working for us since last year, when there weren't any other extra workers available in the hall. They would probably be alright if we employed them."

This is a very strong local, with virtually all of its jurisdiction organized; it is unlikely that many employers would or could put up much resistance to straight down the board hiring which would send them Negro and Mexican workers. However, the local leadership, dependent only upon the international hierarchy, has little reason to make such changes. Instead, it allows minorities to be fired from the industry and, thus, to disappear from the union's membership.

Asked if they thought employment practices should be changed in their industry, they usually said no. "I don't see how you could improve it in any way." A BA summed up his view of the minority group problem.

> "There's surprisingly little resentment to Negroes and Mexicans on the job, unless we send them to a company that hasn't been using them. Then they say, "What the

hell, are you sticking them down our neck?" Once they work in a place there's little resentment. But I don't think the unions should delve into the race question too much; you make an issue out of it and then you have your white boys, some from the South, getting mad at you and they make an issue of it. If you're strictly neutral you stay out of hot water."

The exact effects of such strict neutrality are apparent. Officials believe it is not the union's function to tell the employer whom he can hire, with the result that the employers practice selective hiring and lay-off and eliminate ethnic members hired during periods of labor shortage. Such local leadership, falling in the category Northrup names "laissez faire on the race issue," tends to be over-sensitive to the employer's preference; this does not have to be very strong for the local to acquiesce. Once union and management alike are committed, the situation is structured and resistant to change.

Responsiveness of Leadership to Ethnic Issues:

In a local whose leadership is effectively protected from the members the leaders dominant concern is with international policy and, secondarily, management. For such locals to become active factors in changing ethnic job placement, there must be pressure from one of these two sources. If management wants ethnic workers, the local will be glad to oblige; if there are no other workers available it will send ethnic members out, but only with the consent of management. "When we couldn't get men, we had to let the contractors hire whoever they could."

There is some evidence that pressure at the international level might be effective with such unions. In one International-dominated Craft local, a Negro had been offered a card if he could pass a trade test. The trade test is not often used in such locals; as the BA remarked, "White boys and Mexicans have a good chance to short-circuit the test by working as a 'half-journeyman' and then going on in as a journeyman; the colored guys can't do this."

The Negro refused to take the trade test, protesting that it was used in a discriminatory fashion. According to the BA:

"He had an attorney, the next thing you knew. I went in to see the attorney and he told me the guy was being discriminated against by having to take a trade test. Now I could prove that wasn't so right here in the local; I went back through our books and found we had given a trade test that same year. Well, all the same he wouldn't take the test. The next thing I know, we're

> being sued. I got a letter from the International, saying the NAACP was putting pressure on at the International level."

The N.A.A.C.P. finally abandoned the case on its merits, according to the BA (apparently the Negro was not a competent craftsman) but the Negro carried it to court and cost the local over $1000 in attorney's fees. Since this was the money of the membership, and since a majority of the members are ethnic, there was a sharp reaction.

The international appointed BA made no secret of his dislike for the trouble and expense, as well as the adverse publicity, which the case had entailed-- even though the local had won the verdict. While he was far from "liberal" on the race issue, he went to great length in establishing his International's liberal policy. Such a leader is vulnerable through his International; he is dependent upon the hierarchy for tenure, and he is expected to prevent embarassment for the upper echelons.

Summary:

Most of these locals have contingents of ethnic members who are not represented in the power-structure of the local. The laissez faire policy is standard and the entire decision as to ethnic job-opportunities is given to management, even when the ethnic workers have already gained a substantial foot-hold in the work force. Such locals, with captive members and freedom from coercion by other unions, will change their ethnic members job-status only as a result of pressure from management or from the international hierarchy.

CAPTIVE CRAFT LOCALS

These locals have very heavy concentrations of Mexicans and Negroes, for they control the low-pay, low status, jobs. Such unions do a great deal of their organizing from the top down, with the aid of other and more powerful internationals. A typical example of such organization occurred when a huge new apartment project was being completed. The staff man for a Captive local explained the work force's union affiliation.

> "Whose jurisdiction is it? Well, it was all pre-negotiated, a joint deal with the (names several locals, Captive and Craft). I don't know exactly how it came out, but we got some. Jackson handled it. He wasn't very satisfied. Oh, he got a little above the prevailing rates."

It should be noted that the workers of this enterprise were organized before they had ever thought of getting the job. This is the meaning of pre-negotiation. Such contracts do not fall under the National Labor Relations Board's jurisdiction.

This kind of organizing does not necessarily imply any concern for the workers' consent to membership.

> "Well, our strategy at first was to go to them, talk, educate, try to persuade them. But a lot of people in the local figured this would take too long and wouldn't work out anyway.
>
> "Hell, you've got to understand that all the time we were persuading, you'd have the unorganized feeding on our members and the whole thing could collapse if we didn't get a pretty solid organization. So what we did was ask the (ally) union to help. Those boys had their service outfits organized and wouldn't let the union service them if they didn't belong to our union too.
>
> "But you pay. There's a lot of resistance. It made them mad of course. So I don't know..."

The staff member's own ambivalence concerning this strategy reflects his commitment to the union <u>mystique</u> of solidarity and protest, as well as the basic danger of losing the members' consent. However, his justification is simple and was repeated in different forms many times over.

> "Well, you take a membership like ours; the lowest of the skills and scattered all over the County in little crews. As long as there's any labor at all we can be replaced. So we have to depend on the other unions when we get in a jam to help us out. They can help a lot; if <u>they</u> won't deliver the goods you can shut a place down pretty damned quick."

There is still a need for person to person organizing, for the leadership of these locals, having little strike power without strings attached, have only their members' support as a base of power. One BA describes his work in a difficult situation.

> "That strike we lost let in a lot of scabs-- ah, that strike. You see, Taft-Hartley was in effect when we went back to work so the company couldn't fire the scabs for fear of unfair labor practice charges. We made a deal with them to slowly fire them on one count or another and put our men back on.

"I wish you could have seen how our guys went back to work, one or two at a time, perfectly disciplined, there were no riots-- and you know most of the scabs were white and our men mostly Negro. But boy-- that was a job.

"We have about one-fourth scabs now. And let me tell you about our educational work. In less than a year after the strike was over we had a union shop election and the powerful unions who rode through that strike lost their elections. We won with a one hundred per cent 'Yes" vote! And mind you, that included those scabs.

"How did I work? General Membership meetings, literature in the mails, letters with my signature, buttonholing. It damn near wore me out, glad-handing around. We explained to every man in the local what was up."

Thus the membership of such a local has importance to the leaders in some situations (and to some leaders, as the one quoted above, in many situations). Yet the power of the local leadership depends chiefly upon its organizational allies.

Participation and Representation:

Participation rates are low in these locals when they are very large, as in all craft-type locals. The distance from work to the hall was given, over and over, as an excuse by the leaders. "Our members come to me and say, 'Hell, Bill, by the time I get home from the job, bathe and eat, I'm worn out and it's just too late to get down to the hall.' We don't like it, but I can understand it." However, where the locals are small, amounting to a few hundred members, participation is apt to be high.

Mexicans and Negroes are majorities of all these locals. Their participation in meetings is above average and at the Special Election meetings they are dominant quantitatively. This is reflected in their hold on leadership positions. These are the craft-type locals in which they are well represented on the executive board and, of the three locals studied intensively, two had Mexican and Negro staff members (the other local had only one staff man).

Such ethnic officers may be the result of (1) official cooptation where the local is ruled by a cadre (2) widespread participation under the sponsorship of a democratically minded staff or (3) intensive political agitation along ethnic lines. All three situations were encountered.

1. A member of the staff, describing Mexican and Negro

leaders, said:

> "Well, we usually have to put out a slate for those jobs. You see, people are very reluctant to run for office, especially your minority people. They figure, 'Well, I'm a Negro and nobody will vote for me.' "

Staff control can sometimes result in increasing the membership of ethnic individuals in the control apparatus through ethnic nepotism. "We have three Mexican members on the executive board; you see, our Head Organizer is part Mexican and he has lots of family."

2. In another local with widespread participation, the executive board is always at least one-half ethnic in composition. The president of the local is also a Negro. Ethnic representation results from the larger proportion of the membership Mexican and Negro, and the participating at an average rate. There was little evidence of staff manipulation-- in fact, the president has attacked the non-ethnic staff before the executive board. The board, of which a majority was Negro, defeated him and the incidents "blew over." Should the president have a "legitimate beef" it is not at all certain the staff would not suffer.

An Ethnic Uprising:

In one massive local where there is little participation in General Membership meetings there is nevertheless a large turn-out for elections. This local, predominantly ethnic, was "lily white" in staff and office personnel until recently. In the past few years a temporary dispatcher, a man of unusual sensitivity and intelligence, has risen to a position of leadership. In the process, the face of the local's leadership group was changed.

> "We have a pretty well mixed staff but that's just in the last two years. It used to didn't work that way. Why, when I came in three years back, they had a window in the front and one in the back. The Mexicans, which was most of that membership, would come in holding their caps and sneak around to that back window, pay their dues and leave without saying anything.
> "I asked them, 'What the devil's going on here. Is this the way things are done?' And they said, 'Yes sir, that's the way we do it; we're supposed to come in and pay our dues and get out.' I asked them how it was as far as working, 'Oh, we get work. But sometimes the directions are not too good and we have trouble

reading a new work order.' I asked them if it would help if they had a man who could speak Spanish and explain things better. They thought so. So I asked the Boss to change the arrangements. He said, 'Hell, are you crazy? You don't have Mexican dispatchers!' And that's the issue I ran on for Manager of the local."

The campaign was waged on ethnic lines and, since a majority of the local was ethnic, the new candidate had an advantage. He won by a handy margin; however, in destroying the old leadership's control of the local he created self-conscious ethnic factions. This resulted in a large number of Mexican and Negro candidates for the staff jobs-- sixty per cent in the last election. The staff of the local is now dominated by Negro and Mexican leaders.

Job-protection:

In these Captive craft locals the composition of the membership encourages ethnic leadership; if the local has autonomy and if the ethnic members are self-conscious, they are certain to have an effect on the union's control structure. The ability of such a union to change the job status of ethnic workers will vary, however, with the union's control of the jobs. In the local described above, a number of important changes were made.

"When I came in as Manager we used to have all those systems-- blue card for Negroes, red card for whites, yellow card for Mexicans-- with the foremen calling for the color he wanted. I still remember the first time I got such a call, from a guy in a part of the town where the population is mostly Mexicans. The BA, a Mexican, had been supplying this guy on the q.t. with all-Mexican crews, not clearing them through the hall or anything. Then, when the BA quit, the guy didn't know what to do. So he called me up, 'Yes sir,' I told him, 'This is just the place to call.' Well, he wanted a gang of twelve and he wanted them all Mexican. He'd been getting fine men and they were all Mexicans. I said, 'Yes, we'll send you twelve men Monday.'

"Well, at that time we had ninety-eight per cent Negroes in the hall here, out of work. And I didn't like the idea of sending out a segregated crew anyway -- so I worried about what to do. It was Friday and I had the week-end to worry. I finally talked it over with my wife and (That's funny in a way. I was green. Today I wouldn't bother even to think about it--just go ahead)... Well, anyway, I made up my mind. So the next Monday I picked out twelve damned fine colored guys and I told them just what the score was. 'Boys, it's a problem; but if you just stick together, why I think we're going to solve this thing.'

"Well sir, I didn't hear from that guy for four days; then he called me up. 'If I'd had you on my job Monday morning,' he said, 'I'd have killed you for sure. I asked for Mexicans and here come twelve coal-black smokes! But I want to thank you; those are the best twelve men I ever had-- good workers and good team workers.' I said, 'Well, I expected you to call up and raise old hell.' He said, 'No sir; but I'll tell you what. I need four more men; send me out four Negroes.' I stopped a minute, then I said, 'No we don't; I'll send you out four men, but they'll be damned good men.' 'Alright, fine,' he said. And he's used them mixed up ever since; he still talks about that time, too."

The same situation which results in employer preferences' deciding the issue may thus be used to change the hiring patterns. But it requires courage. It may be hazarded however, that this leader had better reasons and more support for breaking the pattern than would the leaders in the International-dominated local described earlier.

Since the Captive locals control only one job ordinarily, they can do little except attempt to distribute the work equitably. The simplest way is, in theory, simply to force or encourage the use of mixed crews as in the example above; however, curious problems arise from this in some locals.

"The main way our employers discriminate is to call and say they want all white or they want only colored. Where it's an old set up, that's all right, but where it's a new contract we don't like it.

(Question: What about old set ups?)

"Well, we can't force mixing without mixing our colored crews and we've got a lot of all colored crews. You see, our colored members are more likely to be out of a job than the white ones are.

"Some of these old set-ups are very strange. Like the night shift in one place is all colored and the day shift is all white. One company, a Southern outfit, hires only colored. One public market has all colored, but the building above it has all white. Then there's the Pacific Oil Company-- they have all mulatto, sorta beige."

(Question: What can you do about segregated crews?) "Well, as a practical matter, our proportion of unemployed runs heavier for colored than white and we don't discourage the employers from hiring all colored because we got to protect their jobs where they've got them. When we try to change things-- well, sometimes we get a call and use a little vaseline and it'll work in some cases. But we don't really object to all-colored plants. The all-white ones we do. We have mixed crews in many large outfits-- they let us mix them up during the war and now they stick to it."

It is difficult for such locals to use strike power in changing crew selection, since they can usually win only when their allies accept the strike as justified. The allies, having no effective ethnic representation in their locals, are not sympathetic to such strikes. The locals frequently have to persuade their management to change voluntarily. An examply of a staff member's use of persuasion in affecting promotion occurred in one local.

"Theoretically we have a say in promotion to supervision. We have a clause in our contract saying 'Due consideration will be given to seniority, though final discretion is in the hands of the employer. All vacancies must be posted.' Then if the union objects to the selection they must reconsider.

"Now we had an opening for gang boss the other day, on the night shift. There were two whites on the crew and one was a woman. I went down to talk to them about it and they said, 'Well, we've selected Schwartz as the new gang boss.' The one white man on the crew!

"I really blew my top. 'What in the devil are you trying to do?' I asked him. 'Here we've been giving you the best service you've ever got; the department has run like a clock. If you do this it will blow up the whole shift and the whole department. You can't do a thing like this. That man hasn't the seniority of half dozen of the other men. Why are you doing it?'

"They said, 'Well, we think Schwartz is the most qualified. He is honest, intelligent, capable of giving and taking orders.'

"I said, 'Isn't Smith (a Negro) honest?' They said he was. 'Isn't he intelligent and capable of giving and taking orders?' 'Yes.' 'Then why don't you put him on?' Well, they thought the other guy was <u>more</u> qualified.

" 'Look,' I said, 'a seniority clause means the <u>oldest</u>

> man who is qualified-- not the most qualified. If you were to use that method of upgrading there'd be no sense in a seniority system!'
> "Well, the Personnel Manager agreed with me, but he couldn't let his Supervisor down. They had already made their decision, even though they're supposed to post forty-eight hours before they inform the union and withhold decision for thirty-six hours after informing us. They said they would wait to decide.
> "Then I went to the shift and said, 'I want every man on this shift to apply for gang boss!' Well, all but two did. Yesterday they appointed Jones, a damned good man, hard working and <u>colored.</u>"

Such changes, based upon the union's concern for the common law of unionism, are not negligible, though they must cumulate over a long period to affect the basic structure of employment. In these locals the sudden change by fiat of the union is the exception; still, the commitment to change on the part of the leaders can, as in the case above, "make a real difference."

Responsiveness of Leaders to the Issue:

These leaders are limited in their actions, however, by the number and kinds of jobs in their jurisdiction and by the meagre strike power of the locals. One young leader, a liberal, asked why the local didn't enforce its anti-discrimination contract clause, replied:

> "Hell, what can we do? We're just a trade union. We can't do much. Of course there's that contract provision, but there's also the 'ability to perform' clause and the thirty day trial period the employer has.
> "We can't fight discrimination as an unfair labor practice because we're trying to stay out of the jurisdiction of the Taft-Hartley law-- once you get mixed up in there you never get untangled. It will stop you from sympathy strikes, even from organizing strikes! Well, the truth is that if we were under Taft-Hartley we could do a hell of a lot better for our minority members than we do now-- but it would endanger the union.
> "You got to remember that a trade union has to fight for existence and its existence depends on simple commercial things-- wages, hours and working conditions. We can't affort to fight for equality <u>instead</u> of these things; we got to get these things first or we'd go under as an organization."

Such locals are continually struggling for organizational existence, caught between their lack of strategic position in the work flow on one hand and powerful allies on the other. A first condition for staying afloat is help from powerful allies in sympathy strikes (which are frequently also organizing strikes) and in return the local pays a great deal. It is influenced or controlled in matters ranging from political endorsements to contract provisions; even the selection of hired staff is not free from the interest and influence of outsiders. (You know, when we first hired Negro girls in our office force the other unions simply raised hell. 'What in the devil,' they said, 'Nobody ever heard of a Negro girl in an office!' ") Whether such pressures evoke compliance or not they are always factors to be considered.

As one liberal remarked, "The job, of course, is not to be dominated; it's a fine and narrow line you have to walk. Personally, I get along alright with the power boys, but they're a suspicious lot." Another, discussing the problems of operating in this situation, added, "Well, I suppose one of the things I like about this job is the struggle to retain integrity while using the force of such outfits."

The attitudes of professional leaders in these locals were generally favorable to ethnic participation in the union. They are committed to changing hiring practices where they have segregated crews or barriers to foreman jobs for Mexican and Negro members. They may have a considerable effect in changing these work conditions. The amount and type of ethnic participation in leadership varies, but even when control is autocratic the ethnic members are represented, in all leadership positions. Within the limits delineated, the unions can allow ethnic minorities participation on equal status in the union association, can increase job opportunities and make promotion possible for them by enforcing seniority provisions. Such action will usually be the result of persuasion and the extension of the common law of work, rather than force or threat. The use of force is contingent on aid from powerful allies.

MEMBERSHIP-DOMINATED LOCALS I: HALL-ORIENTED

These unions are strong organizationally. Their internal political organization, however, stops at the level of the membership as a whole meeting in the union halls. There is no plant-unit system and participation of the members at General Membership meetings is very low. The proportion of leadership positions held by Negroes and Mexicans is scanty indeed; although they range from one-third to two-thirds of the total membership in all cases, they are under-represented on all executive boards and many contingents have no representation at all.

This does not mean that the paid staff is not dependent upon the membership as a whole for tenure; it does, however, indicate the "mass" nature of the electorate. Because of the weak representation system such locals are vulnerable to control by the machines of the paid staff, to demagoguery, or charismatic leaders. The staff is either independent of the members, through its control of cadres, or it is responsible to factions which represent the rank and file in a very erratic fashion.

Job-protection:

The latter situation occurs in one local with a heavy Mexican contingent and many Negroes. In this local the large executive board does not include a single member of either ethnic contingent-- it is, in fact, dominated by "Texans and other southerners who are against the mixing of the races." The manager of the local is a well-known champion of minorities and a member of the NAACP. However, his efforts to help the Negro members are, in the long view, of questionable effect.

> "They took our young men away yet we were responsible for important war work, so we turned in desperation to the colored. When the war was over the large companies were the first to begin to fire them and the war's been on between them and me ever since.
> "But we did something-- we created a stevedoring division in the union and that is composed of ninety-eight per cent colored men. The other few colored members are scattered throughout the plants. The stevedoring jobs are mostly casual; they call for labor and we send it out."

The contract this local signs prohibits discrimination, yet there are no Negro members at high job levels. Asked about this, the manager responded, "There's no way I can make an employer upgrade a man. The ability to perform clause is staring you in the eye all the time."

This manager, concerned and defensive about his "minority problems," finally concluded, "I think the solution of this thing is a strong apprenticeship system with step by step promotion." He has been able to influence employers to take a number of Negro and Mexican apprentices. However, his solution is quite irrational; there is no chance that the industry, large and highly rationalized, will ever rely upon apprenticeship excepting in small shops where it is frequently used "to beat the journeyman's scale." His reason for emphasizing his apprenticeship program is probably his general impotence to protect Negro job opportunities, aside from saving the casual, low level, labor jobs for them. This impotence stems, in turn, from his dependence upon the racist faction in his executive board and the management opposite him. When he was asked if he thought the employment practices in his industry should be changed, he replied:

> "No, I don't think so. I think our industry is good and considerably better than others. The discrimination is of a local nature that I can fight myself. I don't think it could be changed."

This individual is not in favor of ethnic discrimination, nor is he consciously dishonest; he does have difficulty in squaring his ideology with his actions as a part of the local's organization.

Job Segregation and Ethnic Protest:

There is a similar segregation of Negroes and/or Mexicans at low job levels in most of these Hall-oriented locals. In one local (then a CIO affiliate) the secretary protested at length that there was no discrimination against Negroes or Mexicans, yet there was a very small contingent of the former and both populations were at low job levels. When it was pointed out that job opportunities are scarce for these workers, and it is surprising more of them were not employed in the industry if there was no discrimination, he explained:

> "The company uses a quota system for the different national and racial groups. Well, in proportion to the number of customers in the County from that group, more or less. There's a quota system in the personnel office. But we never have believed into going into 'discrimination in reverse' either. Like the damned Party Boys. We don't make race an issue."

Neither Mexicans nor Negroes are represented in the control system of the locals. Mexicans are limited to physical work, Negroes to janitor jobs. This staff was also quite satisfied with the employment practices in the industry. "Our company doesn't discriminate against anybody. No, I don't think employment should be changed."

It is not surprising that in each local there was clear evidence of discrimination against Negroes and Mexicans in both employment and upgrading practices. The complacency of the local leaders was striking.

> "This here discrimination thing that's always poppin' up, I think I understand it. Now I had a case where the maintenance man in a plant, a white guy, had a colored helper and he loaned him fifty bucks and the colored guy skipped out and never showed again.
> "Well, he was pretty sore and he went to the foreman and said he needed a helper but he didn't want no colored guy. The janitor, black as the ace of spades (and a prince of a fellow) spread the word. Well, the upshot is the foreman calls me and says, 'Ed's got to go, Jack; I'm sorry, because he's a good man but he's got to go.' I said, 'Whatsa matter?' He said, 'Well, he said he didn't want no Negro helper and the colored guys is all threatening to walk off if he don't leave tomorrow. I can't have that.'
> "Well, I said to him, 'Hell no, Ed stays.' He says, 'OK, but you'd better get your ugly face down, because if you don't I'll be in one hell of a jam tomorrow.'
> "Well, I went right down to the plant, caught 'em after work, and there they were, off in a sort of a group, throwin' their chests out and lookin' real sassy. I said to 'em, 'Now you say you're going to walk off your job, is that right?' They said, 'yes.' 'What the hell, that's crap! You'll do no such of a thing, you hear me?' They muttered something about how they was being discriminated against. I said, 'God damn it to hell, now you listen to me! What did Ed say? Did he say he didn't want no NIGGER working for him?' They said he hadn't. 'Did he say he didn't want no JIGABOO?' They said no. 'He said he didn't want no <u>colored</u> guy. Now is it discrimination to call you colored guys? Hell, some of you get mad when you're called jigs or niggers or colored or Negroes-- Now what the hell, the guy has to call you something.'
> "They said, 'We're going off though, because the guy has discriminated.'
> "I said, 'You listen to me; you're going to do no such of a thing. Listen, you kinkyheaded sons of bitches, you know if you walk off that job tomorrow your names'll be mud? You know the word'll go down the district so fast your heads will swim? Every god-damned foreman and colored guy on the street will know it and what'll happen? Everyone that don't like you will pour it on. You'll all begin getting fired-- because there's men out of work."

The Negro workers went back to work, but it is doubtful if the leader ever understood their objections to Ed's behavior. Their only recourse, however, political action within the local, is very difficult, for this leader has a powerful sway over the members and is a good trade unionist as well- an able man who "brings home the bacon" at contract negotiations.

Ethnic Representation:

The ethnic workers' lack of an organizational position from which they could force such a leader to understand their problems is a key to their defeat in the incident recounted above. There are no Negroes or Mexicans in any official position in the local and Negroes are excluded from several departments in the industry. However, where they have jobs and seniority, the jobs are protected; this local is strong and the seniority clause applies to all members.

In only two of these locals do Negroes have substantial representation in the control system and in these locals they are, in effect, cadres for the paid leadership. A staff member of one local describes the procedure. "The officers are elected from stacked ballots, 'The Slate' as it's called, and the leaders use the Negroes as fronts to increase their own support."

Such coopted ethnic leaders have little effect as ethnic representatives; they represent the paid staff first, their fellow ethnic members second. The average job level of Negroes was below average in each local, though there was no evidence that they did not get standard union protection on the job otherwise.

Summary:

The leaders of Hall-oriented locals are either protected from the ethnic issue or use one ethnic minority as a cadre to guarantee its hold on the large, "massified," membership. Leaders uniformly accept hiring practices and promotional practices in their industries as fair, although such practices penalize ethnic union members. Change in the status of ethnic members, in the union and on the job, comes about through (1) political organization in the local or (2) direct pressure on management through "wildcat strikes." The first is difficult, due to the problems of organizing rank and file strength in such locals; the second is dangerous for the reasons pointed out by the local leader quoted earlier.

MEMBERSHIP-DOMINATED LOCALS II: PLANT-ORIENTED

These locals also have independent strike power. They are exposed to their membership (1) in the general sense that strike power originates in the entire membership and (2) in the specific sense that the plant-unit organization gives the members a closer control over their officers, through an organizational middle class. Participation is high for Mexicans and Negroes, and where they are as much as one-tenth of the members they are uniformly represented on the executive board of the local. They are proportionally represented as stewards and, frequently, in staff positions. There was no evident cooptation of ethnic leaders among these locals. Mexicans and Negroes are fully represented in the internal political structure of these locals.

Effect of Representation on Ethnic Protest:

Such representation, however, does not automatically result in their determining policy, nor does union success in protecting the jobs of ethnic members always follow. The leaders of these locals were the most frank in discussing cases of company discrimination against their ethnic members. Such discrimination was, in fact, part of the union's armoury of weapons to use against the company; the union protest motif and the ethnic protest were parallel, if not identical, in the thinking of these officers. And, in each local there was some formal structure meant to decrease discrimination against minority members. The representation of Mexicans and Negroes in the power structure of the locals (1) increased the pressure on the staff to make race an issue and (2) yielded the elected officers political support for such a position.

An officer in one local indicates such a formal structure.

> "We have a Fair Employment Committee in our plant that's really strong. Maybe it's not impressive, but these are the details that make democracy possible. We had a man who wanted to be transferred to another department that was all white; he hadn't been able to get transferred. We put a little pressure on management through the Committee and got him in. The same thing in another transfer case. The hell of it was, in one instance -- the foreman of the department where the guy wanted to go, a white guy, was his friend and he only had to learn the guy wanted in to accept him."

In such cases, the mere existence of formal machinery helps to clarify the ambiguous situations that result, for in tracing the origins of particular ethnic barriers, it is frequently a case of "button, button, who's got the button?" and nobody has it; the button does not exist. Associated with this ambiguity is the situation where management and workers have no particular position, but lower level supervision has been able to determine policy by default. "If you pressure a personnel man, you'll soon find out if it's him or management that wants discrimination; I'd sooner try to get close to one than to the actual management." (Personnel officers frequently bear the brunt of accusations by union leaders where discrimination is concerned.)

These locals usually have non-discrimination clauses in their contracts. They are taken seriously when the relative power of the local _vis a vis_ the company allows this.

> "We never had colored people out in the foothill area -- Pasadena, Alhambra, Azusa. We've finally settled that. It was all right when we finally decided to do it. After all, there it is on our contract and we had a water tight case before the NLRB. We have also cracked Huntington Park, which was lily white-- got fifteen Filipinos in there now."

The leaders of these locals, exposed to and representing a membership that includes many Mexicans and Negroes is, of necessity, uniformly favorable to changing hiring practices in the various industries. "Certainly they should be changed, especially for the colored people." Their opinion is usually that both government action and union action should be taken. Only in the very strong locals with union-shop contracts is there a variation; "Get a strong FEPC clause in the contract and enforce it."

Ethnic Protest Versus Democratic Processes:

It may be said that race is an issue in each of these locals. It is an issue that is out in the open and one which the leaders struggle with, both in their "foreign relations" and in their internal politics. The results are not always favorable to ethnic contingents, however; when the membership is represented in the seat of power, the racist members may also be heard.

An example occurred in a CIO local with a heavy proportion of Mexican and Negro members. The leaders of the local had been elected on a fair employment practices platform; the president of the local describes the inter-ethnic conflict.

> "We have a lily-white department and I've started work to have that changed. I told the members of the department and they listened in stony silence. But later (listen, it'll give you an idea) a friend of mine and a damned good union guy came up to me and said, 'Listen, they tell me you're telling those niggers to come down and get jobs with us. Well, listen; we have

> an industry agreement and all of us at our plants have decided we won't let the niggers in. If they do come in we'll shut the plant down.'
>
> "I told him, 'You've got no right to do any such thing. You know our constitution and our contract and our international policy are all dead set against it.'
>
> "He said, 'Listen boy, this thing is too big for you and you had better leave it alone.' "

To understand further developments, the position of the union's regional leader must be understood. This leader was himself from an ethnic minority; his international hierarchy had originally sponsored him for his post but he still had to validate himself with the various locals and was very cautious. Organization within the plant varied, though most of the industry was under contract, but the local had stiff competition from its AFL counterpart. The balance of power between ethnic and non-ethnic members varied from local to local in the region; in the local described above, the organization was chiefly Negro, but in another larger and more important plant a group of whites controlled the union and retained control through an "anti-Negro" program.

The president of the local, who was trying to break down ethnic barriers in the "lily-white" department, ran into strong opposition in his plant for the white workers were organized into a faction with members from the "lily white" department as leaders; they expressed solidarity in the meetings through their statements and votes. Each ethnic faction had its spokesmen, who were in opposition most of the time; the leadership supported the Negroes, while the company gave tacit support to the white workers. The president, interviewed some time after his campaign had begun, gave this progress report.

> "You know, I'm getting a little worried. The company has a stooge following me on my trips and I already got laid off a week. What happened was they called me up one day and said I hadn't made my trips fast enough. Well, I had been deliberately hurrying and I'm fast as hell anyway. But they come up with this kind of thing: 'On August 21, you took twenty minutes at this stop; on September 30, forty minutes at that stop' and so on. Well, hell, there's not much you can do in a situation like that. So I made a grievance out of it when they laid me off.
>
> "The grievance meeting was pretty soon and here's Jack (the regional director) and he listens to them and he says: 'Well, I can see there's some legitimate cause for protest against the work here; suppose we compro-

mise on a three day lay-off.' The company agreed. "I was mad as Hell! Jack went off talking about what a moral victory we had gained. I told him it was no such of a damned thing."

This company oriented behavior on the part of the ethnic-identified regional director who was sympathetic to the president's program, who was his personal friend, and who was aware that he had been framed because of trouble making on the color issue, must be understood in the context of the regional leader's sources of power. The president went on:

"Of course I know what Jack is doing. He's strengthening himself with that faction in the union that thinks we ought not to mess with FEPC. The white guys say it's a waste of the union's time."
(Are the Negroes and Mexicans behind you?)
"They're the ones who voted me in as president, but the votes split then on a color line."
(Do you think Jack will let the Company saw you off the limb?)
"I don't know. He might. He thinks of himself as a shrewd politician and there's been some resistance to the action I've been getting."

This was the reaction of the members in the "lily-white" department when their president and co-worker reported the manner in which he had been framed.

"Well, they all got together in the lunch room and said the charges were a load of crap; but they were a little unsure of themselves because of my trying to break the 'lily-white' rule in the department.
(Would they stand by you if the company decided to fire you?)
"Well, I don't know. I do know that the company is mainly interested in me because of the FEPC program we've got going now."

This, of course, was the reason the white workers had for being uncertain about him. The split in the membership on ethnic issues can be used by anyone, including the management opposite the local, as a weapon for attacking union leaders. This man was fired a month later, on charges similar to those described above. He reported:

"I'm not working at the plant anymore. It was pretty fishy too, I can tell you. My case is in arbitration,

> but that takes months. I'm afraid it's lost-- you see, Jack is lousy at arbitration. He loses ninety per cent of his cases."

Yet the director who has been called "Jack" could not go too far in repressing the ethnic protest, for the industry had a large number of Negroes and Mexicans, over half the total membership, and they were well represented in the official hierarchy of the locals--source of rival leaders. It must be remembered that the member of the organizational middle-class, the president of the local, had broad support as well as broad opposition. He was eliminated only through a combination of management, the racist faction, and his regional director's passive attitude.

Summary:

Mexicans and Negroes participate much more intensively in the control structure of these locals and their influence is felt by the paid staff. This staff, in turn, is committed to improving job conditions for ethnic workers and uses a number of means in attempting this. Change in such locals is chiefly a function of the relative strength of company and union. However, the proponents of change do not always win out-- there are many discrepancies between the ideal of equal treatment and the empirical possibilities. In some cases, as in the last described above, the anti-equality factions in the membership exert more influence on the local leadership (in combination with the management opposite) than do the ethnic groups-- for they also will be represented in a control structure based upon membership consent.

THE RACE ISSUE IN FOUR TYPES OF LOCAL: A COMPARISON

Investigation of the conditions under which race is an issue, and the outcome of the issue, in each of these four types of locals, shows clear-cut differences by type of local. These stem from differences in the status of the ethnic contingent on the job and in the local, while the way the issue is resolved further affects status.

In the International-dominated locals the question of raising or lowering barriers to ethnic participation is rarely important. Pressure from the members affects the issue only if it is directed at management or the international, for the leaders of these locals are insulated from the opinions and interests of their members. However, pressure from either the international hierarchy or management will affect the leadership. In general, ethnic contingents in the local do not affect policy and they are hired and fired at the will of management.

In the Captive locals ethnic contingents tend to participate in the control structure of the local. The leaders may be insulated from the members or exposed to them-- generally leaders control the elections through a cadre. However, since ethnic workers are such large proportions of the memberships, a rebellion on ethnic lines is possible if effective cooptation does not exist. These unions attempt to equalize job status for ethnic members through (1) mixing crews and (2) supporting ethnic members for upgrading. They usually cannot force these results; their strike power is borrowed and they must use persuasion.

In the Membership-dominated locals, where the members are the direct source of strike power and the leaders are dependent on their vote for job tenure, the race issue will exist wherever a significant proportion of the members are of ethnic identity. The issue may be latent or overt, however, depending upon the availability of political means of expression. In the Plant-oriented locals, where the members have access to the decision-making process and the leaders are exposed to the members, the race issue will be a live issue indeed. In such locals the leaders are in favor of integration and tend to take action (though limited action) in this direction.

In other locals of comparable ethnic composition, but Hall-oriented politically, the issue is latent. Such locals allow the paid leadership much more freedom from commitment on the subject. The leaders usually accept the going pattern (though with some misgivings) and reinforce it through their organizational policy. Minorities have little effect on the political situation in such locals, though they are occasionally used as a cadre for the leaders.

When ethnic issues are raised in a local, the splits in the electorate may be reinforced by pressure from outside the local's political system-- the international hierarchy, other unions, or management. The resolution of the issue within the local may then reflect the relative importance of the various sources of power to the local leadership, rather than the feelings of membership or leadership on the merits of the issue. The end result will be tested by the consent of the membership, however, in the Plant-oriented locals.

Two major factors are discernible in the status of ethnic members in the union and on the job. One is the ethnic composition of the local, the other, the degrees of political freedom which the individual members of the local are allowed by the structure of the organization. The probability of successful union action for an ethnic minority, however, against major barriers to employment, is severely limited by the power position of the local as an organization.

One may see three concentric sets of limits upon "what can be done about race" in a given local union. The first are the necessary conditions for the existence of the local; the second, in large part derived from this, the degrees of freedom the members have in determining union policy through pressure on the leaders; the third, the degree of organization among the "pro ethnic" union members-- ordinarily members who are, themselves, of ethnic identity (though not always so). In a local union with a large proportion of ethnic members, _if_ the local is not captured by the international or its leadership, and _if_ the ethnic members have organization and channels of influence, the local "will try to do something for the minority groups." The things the local can do will be limited by its effective power _vis a vis_ its employers. Locals in which the conditions for ethnic pressure are most suitable are industrial locals of the Plant-oriented variety. However, many of the locals with the greatest power are the Craft-type locals-- the ones least apt to take action on ethnic issues.

Of the ethnic union members in these locals, only five per cent are in the International-dominated locals; forty-three per cent are in the Captive locals dependent upon them. Thirty-four per cent are in the Hall-oriented locals with membership domination, twelve per cent in the Plant-oriented locals and six per cent in the one membership-dominated Craft local, the Retail Clerks. Thus most of these members are in the Captive locals (whose power over employers is in the hands of the _laissez faire_ Craft locals) and in the Hall-oriented locals whose ethnic members have little political power. Only in the Plant-oriented locals does the union show a continuous, dynamic policy towards ethnic-based inequalities.

These Plant-oriented locals were with two exceptions, CIO. The AFL locals in this sample were thus divided into the International-dominated, the Captive and the Hall-oriented locals. The conclusion is inescapable that Mexicans and Negroes had better opportunities to use the local as an arena for generating power and changing their status in CIO locals of the sample. This is not so much a result of the ideology of the leadership, however, as a result of organizational structure in the local unions. (The degree to which this structure is a result of ideology is another problem; the point is, that given the structure, these are the results to be expected.) The craft fragmentation of the labor force, common in the AFL, left ethnic minorities concentrated in locals with the least strike power; the sympathy strike which gave them access to power also left them dependent upon the true craftsman's unions. The Hall-oriented locals, originally derived from Craft internationals, were run on a mass-leadership basis which makes realistic pressures from the membership very difficult.

The purpose of this analysis was not to compare the virtues of the two federations, but to illuminate the organizational conditions which are the basis for effective ethnic participation in the union movement. Study of the CIO and left-wing locals with Hall-oriented structures shows clearly that "being CIO" did not guarantee "a better deal for the minority guys". In these locals the same domination by machine obtained as in other Hall-oriented locals, while in the AFL Plant-oriented local the structure allows participation and representation of the rank and file, including the Negro and Mexican rank and file. It was the local's control structure which was decisive, nots its affiliation. Such organizational conditions, resulting in constraint and pressures upon the staff, were the most effective determinants of the local's policies.

CHAPTER VIII

VALUES AND SOCIAL ACTION: DIFFICULTIES OF THE DEVIANT LABOR LEADER

As sociological analysis, this study has been concerned with the "sociological man," the role-player in an organized group intent upon keeping his position and maintaining his organization. The actors in the systems described here had only these attributes: job, ethnic identity, position in a specific local labor union. Such is the nature of sociological explanation; the molecular unit is the social role.

However, in empirical fact, these actors are differentiated in a multitude of ways; their self images, their ideals and ideologies, their rational understanding of "the movement," range from one end of any continuum to the other. The defense of the analysis presented thus far requires a justification of the attributes used, as opposed to such differentiating factors as those noted above. For this reason, as well as for the additional light thrown upon the role system of the local union, the career patterns and action limits of some "deviant" labor leaders will be described in detail.

Ethnic labor leaders and labor intellectuals, with strong commitments to other values than those involved in "keeping a job in the movement," are fit subjects for a test of the determinate power of organizational constraint. It is the contention of this paper that such personal values and commitments are of very little relevance in themselves to the study of the union as an agency of social power. The ability of liberals and ethnics in leadership positions to realize their values is a measure then of the effects to be expected from replacing "bad men" with "good men"-- or poor personnel with able personnel.

SITUATIONAL PRESSURES AND FUNCTIONAL ROLE OF THE ETHNIC LEADER

As noted earlier, twenty-four staff members are of ethnic identity, sixteen Mexican and eight Negro. They constitute approximately one-third of the staff members in the sample. Although they are not a major part of the union leadership in Los Angeles County, their concentration and numbers would seem to make possible some effective pressure upon the unions in the direction of lowering barriers to ethnic employment. There was little evidence that this occurred.

Certain statistics should be remembered. First, Mexican

and Negro leaders are found only in locals with a high proportion of ethnic-identified members (thirty to eighty-three per cent, with the mean at fifty per cent). In the usual case, ethnic leaders have staff positions in locals where their specific ethnic group is a major part of the membership. Second, they are likely to be the only person of their ethnic identity on a large staff. Third, fifteen of these leaders are elected, but nine are appointed. There is no difference in type of tenure by ethnic identity; forty per cent of each group is appointed.

The usual ethnic leader is on a large staff having a majority of "anglos" or whites. He is not usually chosen simply because of his leadership abilities and union identification; he is a minority representative. As such, he serves a special function for the union leadership and for the ethnic contingent in the membership.

Organizational Commitment and Ethnic Commitment:

As the local's ethnic representative, his job is that of gaining and keeping the confidence of Mexican and Negro members and, thus, strengthening the local's organization (15). In order to do this he must profess specifically _ethnic goals_-- but this utility for the local stems from his channelling protest within the organization and not against it. As leader in a protest movement, however, he is subject to the situational pressures of the accommodative leader already noted; he must control ethnic resentment. This he can do only by expressing it, yet the necessities of his position as a union leader force him to continually bargain for small advantages, rather than strike for a showdown. He experiences, in a redoubled form, the situational pressures described for the union leader _sui generis._

If an ethnic leader is appointed, his double responsibility to the "race" and to top leadership will be heavily weighted in favor of the latter. He is responsible first of all to his source of power. Over half the leaders in the Hall-oriented locals are appointed. Such leaders, however, to keep their utility for the union and to satisfy personal commitments, must show responsibility for the ethnic members, though with little power to make decisions affecting them. This type of ethnic leader will be primarily a channel of communication or a "front" for the top leaders.

At the same time he will be exposed to the _esprit de corps_ of the local's leadership-- he will be a member of a small social circle, and will tend to identify with the organization. Thus he will come to see his own responsibilities in terms of his knowledge of the larger organization's problems. As one ethnic leader said, in response to probing on this score:

"You see, you get a great loyalty to the organization in an outfit like this. These guys, they do things and they do things-- and they know it won't wash. They get to a point where they have to say, 'No, I can't justify it on my grounds. I can't justify it on any grounds, but I will do it for my organization. My organization, my union above everything.'
"It's pretty frightening, because then you get your own head taken off by guys who are operating under that same motto."

The appointed leader will thus be very sensitive to any "uprising" which threatens the basic security of the local (and of his own position). Though he may press for gains, they will tend to be small and, organizationally speaking, irrelevant. The most progress can be made within the strictly union structure-- such officers take pride in having Negroes in the steward corps, Mexicans and Negroes out at the picnic and the like. Some progress can be achieved in job status, occasionally. Many craft unions can be made more liberal where apprenticeship is concerned but where "crew selection" by the employer is questioned little can be done. The first does not constitute a real threat to the union's source of power: the second disturbs relations with employers, apt to be crucial for such a local.

The appointed leader is dependent on top leadership and is not committed to ethnic members except through the leader. He does not have an overwhelming need for their support and by the same token cannot affort to gamble his position on such support. He can justify his position by the reflection that, were he fired, the man who succeeded him would face the same dilemma he confronts.

Most ethnic leaders in the Plant-oriented locals are elected; they have a degree of independence the appointed leader cannot know. The leader in such a case is committed to the membership and is likely to be so committed on ethnic lines. He is fully involved in the problems of administration-- of reconciling diverse and fluctuating pressures within a stable framework of commitments. He is likely to be faced with real conflict between his political commitment to "the race" or "la raza" and the commitments a union must make to stay in business. The allies of one high-ranking ethnic leader whose position was described above include (1) communist fractions in his own and other internationals, (2) militant "race men" in his union, (3) a white supremacy group in control of one plant and, (4) the conservative and racist leadership of a competing union in the field. His condition is perenially unstable; his objective actions are so erratic as to provoke the judgement of opportunism, yet he is known as "a real race man at heart."

Each time such a leader admits he is unable to affect the policy of the union or the management contracted he risks some loss of influence among his ethnic constituency. As this happens, he loses his usefulness to the organization and at the same time provides issues for rival race leaders. A common reaction to such a predicament is to emphasize the race issue verbally, while acting in a contrary manner in the course of work. Since, however, a loud ethnic "party line" arouses opposition along ethnic lines, the Negro or Mexican leader then has to deal with a white or anglo faction in his membership. He is in the position of having to rob Peter to pay Paul. Some notion of the effects of these conflicts can be gained from one Negro staff member's remarks.

> "I'm gonna get my head lifted right off my shoulders. When you get right down in the field, boy, the cross-pressures-- the Negro prejudice against whites and the white prejudice against Negroes-- meet in your head and blow the lid off. And that's what you got to take. No wonder the best, most sensitive, people go up where the pressure's not so great, in the top brackets. It's a killer."

Personal Position and Democratic Processes:

Thus far the conflict between organizational commitment and ethnic commitment has been emphasized. It must be remembered that there is another conflict the leader faces: that beween his personal position and democratic processes. In this matter, the position of the ethnic leader is more difficult than most. First, the Mexican and Negro labor forces tend to be concentrated in low status jobs and, second, such ethnic individuals as become leaders are more limited in their job alternatives than are other leaders. Their function is likely to be specialized to union work and to a particular union at that. They lack a negotiable skill, and when they fall, fall far.

These conditions, combined with the greater objective difficulties such leaders experience in keeping their jobs, indicate that the horns of the dilemma are even closer together and sharper for the ethnic leader than for most union leaders. The conflict between a high status job and "the race" is acute. Quotations of statements by Negro union leaders, characterizing other Negro leaders, will illustrate the point.

> "That guy's two men. He joined the Party during the war and maneuvered himself into a key spot, working as a big shot in the X union. He's a good looking, intelligent boy-- and he'll keep his good looks because

he aims to have soft white collar jobs.
"When the war was over and the red scare started, he went over to the Right wing and got a job through them. He's a phony, but then he's not. The other side is he's intensely Nationalistic; he really wants to do something for the Race.
"But he wants comfort and prestige, too."

(It should be noted that to do something for the Race, to become a race hero, is a conventional path to prestige and negotiable publicity for Negroes-- as well as an idealistic commitment.) The man who made the statement quoted above was characterized as follows by another ethnic leader. "He's got a big shot complex that gets him into trouble-- poor bastard."

Another leader was characterized in this manner:

"Smith, my friend, is a man without integrity or honor or intelligence. He is an ass. He is not a bad ass-- in fact he is a good old ass. But he is an ass and nobody respects him. That union uses him for their jim-crow work."

A fellow Negro leader described this commentator:

"Well, I'll tell you about old Rube. He's smart, and he's a pretty good man, too. But he's always thinking of Rube."

Mexican Leaders and Negro Leaders:

Negro leaders are probably subject to more strain between personal status and democratic processes than are Mexican leaders for these reasons: (1) their status alternatives in industry are lower (2) they have access to the rewards of the relatively well-organized Negro community-- a society, a press and a whispering gallery. Evidence indicates a high degree of communication among Negro leaders, which crosses organizational lines. They know one another as people and as mirrors of themselves. The Mexican leaders, on the other hand, seem to be more isolated. From casual checking it appears that few Mexican leaders are personally acquainted with those in other internationals.

The same barriers which limit the Negro leader's alternatives and create extreme occupational hazards for him have the ironic effect of increasing the rewards of his high-status job-- if he can keep it. In contrast, Mexican enclaves in Los Angeles are more loosely organized and Mexican industrial labor has more access to high level jobs.

Because of relatively higher status and lack of status alternatives at the same level, and greater insecurity of tenure, the expected behavior of ethnic leaders includes an increased use of techniques common to all labor leaders in this dilemma: demogoguery, or an appeal to the members as a mass, and the cadre--control through a well organized personal following.

The ethnic leader, with the exception of a very few locals, is isolated from his ethnic fellows in a milieu predominantly white or anglo; he is "up to his ears in work," from which there is no escape, and the work isolates him from larger issues in which he may be interested. Finally, as with all leaders, the conditions for convenience tend to be accepted as necessities; that which can be stabilized is stabilized, at the expense of compromising future action. The personal commitment to the race may be strong-- in general it is among these Negro and Mexican leaders-- but whether it will be of much importance under these conditions is problematical.

In short, the conflicts inherent in the role situation of the labor leader (1) between the protest motif and the accommodation motif and (2) between the technical function and democratic processes, are redoubled in the case of ethnic leaders. This is most severe in the case of the Negro leader, where the protest motif is socially reinforced by the Negro community, while the accommodative motif is strengthened directly by the long tradition of accommodative race leaders and indirectly by his position as something of a "race hero." Yet the Negro leader's technical and political functions are more difficult than those of most leaders, while his valuation of his job is likely to be even higher than theirs.

The extreme case of the Negro union leader illuminates some of the reasons why ethnic labor leaders are not apt to develop much influence on the course of ethnic relations in industry or the locals.

THE LABOR INTELLECTUALS

The second group of leaders who are committed to deviant goals are the labor liberals, or the intellectuals of the movement. These men, who are usually highly educated and who participate in the labor movement for moral reasons, are particularly important as channels by which ideas get into the labor movement and as examples of the futility of ideas without power.

The Ideal of a Political Labor Movement:

Many of them first came into the movement in the 1930's and the ideological importance assigned to the unions by Marxist and reformist theories conditioned their own careers. Today, however, it becomes increasingly apparent that the American worker's definition of labor unions is hardly that of a revolutionary. Images of the good trade unionist and the union guy are not in moral opposition to capitalism; indeed, American unions of any importance are committed to the continuance of the capitalist system-- for the members expect their leadership to sacrifice long-term social goals for "more here and now." Success in this latter enterprise is a basic criterion for the status of a leader and his local.

Thus Communist union leaders must, in the long run, be union leaders first and Communists second. The rebellion in Local "B" indicates this clearly. Asked about the wide support which the Communist leaders had, their organizational opponent answered:

> "They go along mainly because, well, they figure the local has been a good union and always done a good job. They think, 'well, political differences are political but the union has given us a good break.' "

Another leader in the AFL confirmed this in speaking of a Communist dominated local with wide support from its Negro members.

> "The Negroes got a good break there and worked all over the board, which they've never done in most AFL unions. So what do they do? They just block out the idea that the leadership is Communist-- just refuse to accept it."

To be "trade union" first and radical second is, however, to accept the limits on leadership which have been indicated.

The ideologies of a political labor movement, in subordinating immediate economic gains and security to long term historicist trends or long term moral goals, issue in political strikes, draining the treasury, and "taking part in things that are none of the local's business." They run directly counter to the usual function of the American union. They may be tolerated if the "bread and butter" work is accomplished, but they are luxuries. When they prevent the realization of these material goals they are expensive for the leadership in its problems of control.

"Hot-rods" and Trouble-Makers:

At the time of this study most intellectuals who were leaders were in extremely unstable positions. Ten labor liberals-- editors, research and publicity personnel, educational directors and international representatives-- were fired during the two years of the field work. All were fired from liberal organizations. All were to the left of the membership, though none was "left" in the sense of sympathy with the Communist party. They were also to the left of other union leaders, particularly with respect to ethnic issues and democratic processes. One was a representative for a large CIO union.

> "Yeah, I got the treatment since I saw you last. I was fired."
> (Why was that-- how did it happen?)
> "Oh, because I did my job a little too well, I guess. I was a hot rod. Hell, you can't have personal freedom in an organization, I reckon."
> (What came up?)
> "Oh, the usual things. But mainly, I didn't build up my caucus."
> (Was it administrative?)
> "Yeah, but (shrugging) you know how these things are. Political."

A local officer in a CIO union known as a "comer," who was important in the district council and in his international as a minority rights leader, was denied a promised promotion into the Council. Discussing his case, another liberal remarked:

> "Well, I don't know the details-- why he didn't get the job they promised him. I knew he wouldn't though-- and I know why. It was perfectly obvious he was a red hot boy. He would be a trouble maker from the start. So they wouldn't have him."

The trouble maker is one who speaks out of turn, creates problems not necessary to the organization as the "brass" sees it-- the man who embarasses his fellows. Another liberal leader commented:

> "Hell, he got himself tagged, and tagged too early. Then too, you know, he keeps shooting off his mouth and he makes everybody else look bad. Nobody is going to appreciate that."

This man, a young college graduate of ethnic identification, had a meteoric career. His honesty and his direct speech started him as a leader-- and destroyed his career. He falls into the general category of the "crusader type," the outspoken person who consistently takes a principled stand and lets the chips fall where they may. His career illustrates one reason why labor liberals are cautious in their public acts: the chief result of this man's efforts was the elimination of himself from the union movement.

These cases are typical in showing that leaders whose values are far from the mode among their fellow leaders require more political strength to hold a position than does the ordinary trade unionist. This becomes a critical factor when such a leader is active and vocal, thus presenting immediate practical problems for his local and role problems for his fellow leaders.

Organizational Position and Intellect:

Such intellectuals usually have little political strength. Most of them are appointed and are personally dependent upon the real leader who appointed them. In this situation they are very cautious indeed. A good friend explains one man's behavior.

> "You see, Jerry's position is not easy; he's not from a union but just a hired hand. And some of the guys from other unions will say, 'Hell, who's this guy to throw his weight around? He's got no organization behind him. He's just one of Jorgenson's employees.' And Jerry feels that."
> (Why doesn't Jerry have a position?)
> "Well, he has connections. But he's run onto the same thing so many of us have to handle. Most unions have a constitutional requirement that you be a union member three years before you can hold office; so most of the liberals are employees. Jerry has taken out a card in some minor union but *that's* a long way around."

The effects of this political weakness are many; two general courses of action are possible. The leader can follow the examples quoted earlier, strike out for what he believes is best and probably "strike out." Or, being aware of the power structure, he can conform to the shape of his role as it is defined by the organization. It is frequently one which leaves little room for his broader values or theoretical awareness.

> "My job is political action, organizing clubs. Also writing leaflets for pending shops, where we think there's a chance for us to get a foot in the door. Then

> I've got to give a speech tomorrow on why the government needs public relations; I'll have to read a book on that tonight I guess and make a thirty-five minute speech.
> "I was slated for research. I occasionally do a graph if it can be used for a leaflet. But none of these surveys-- I haven't got the temperament for it-- they bore hell out of me. We had a guy in here on research. He went out and told the boys what to do. Lectured them. He didn't last."

This individual was described by a labor intellectual (in a very similar situation) as follows.

> "Those people are intelligent all right-- they're intelligent whores. Jerry's very bright, but he doesn't use his mind to get anywhere."
> (What do you mean, to get anywhere?)
> "To be effective. Yeah, that's right, you get eliminated if you do-- like me for instance."

Asked about the reasons for his own expulsion from leadership, he continued:

> "The beginning of the end though was when I was at a meeting of the council. Andy wasn't there. The director said, 'I guess you've all noticed Andy isn't here. There's a good reason-- Andy's a Communist and we can't have Communists at our meetings.'
> "Well, I got up and said, 'Looky, you've just made a statement about a man, and a pretty serious one. I've never heard it before. The man's not here to defend himself. Suppose you give us a little proof!'
> "Well, he blew up at that. 'Who in Hell are you to tell me what people to have in my council? The thing you've got to learn, my friend, is that you can't work with Communists!'
> "Well, he should be telling me!
> "Look,' I said, 'There's only two guys here who have a right to say that. We were saying it long ago, when everybody else was hand in glove with 'em. <u>You</u> were in bed with them yourself in those days and you stayed in bed until Phil Murray pulled you out. And if he told you to, you'd hop right back in tomorrow.'
> "Well, that's no way to make friends, even if you do influence people. When he did produce the evidence-- it was pitiful."

Such behavior may strengthen democratic processes, but it also causes individuals who lack power to be dropped from the movement. Thus a continual conflict between principle and the realities of power (or 'expediency') produces a great deal of psychological insecurity in such individuals. It is significant that the only staff person to refuse an interview flatly was a labor liberal in a liberal union. Her reasons were transparently false; when pressed, she said, "I'm just a hired hand around here. We people who are not up from the ranks just can't take any chances." This also was one of the few cases where it was evident that an outright lie was told by a respondent.

The intensity of this insecurity is apparent in the remarks of a liberal and an intellectual, a person who had once been an instructor in economics in a major university. This man, out of place in the labor movement, was equally alienated from "do nothing intellectuals." He defined his relations as follows.

> "You take these academic people, I'd say, let them stay in their place, making their living there. Let them (a gesture as if leafing a book) feather their molasses. Goddammit, let them work up from AB to MA to PHD, from Assistant to Associate to Department Head, on their own and make their living out there.
> "Let them stay in their Institutes of Industrial Relations and leave us alone. Then if they want to help Labor on the side, why let them work with us. But my own thinking is, that with a war economy-- a semi-war economy-- it's the same thing-- coming on, the best thing for labor is just to keep ourselves to ourselves. I don't mean pure and simple trade unionism. But I do mean finding the right men for the right jobs, and trying to work out our problems by ourselves. I've always said that if Labor is going to get anywhere it'll have to do it by itself. We'll have to pull ourselves up by our bootstraps."

This individual, so identified with "Labor," was himself an intellectual who had never been a union member or done any manual labor.(He later became friendlier and was of considerable assistance in the study.)

Some individuals have influence, however, upon key leaders. This is probably the chief means by which labor intellectuals can affect policy. "Why is our union as good as it is? Well, I don't know that it's any good. But I'd say top leadership and a few guys like Art and Bill at the low level. We guys have no power but we can get to the top leader." The end effects of such influence are difficult to trace. If there were a coherent policy it would be simpler. In general, one can only call the labor liberal's program one of amelioration, in the general direction of such values as ethnic equality of opportunity, democratic processes, aid for the underpriveleged and political participation through the Democratic party in national elections. Wherever labor liberals have official positions, it is for such things they fight, but the fight is necessarily a quiet and cautious one.

SUMMARY

Deviant labor leaders, ethnics and intellectuals alike, represent an exceptional commitment to certain ideals. Their career patterns in the movement are instructive for, in the locals of this sample, such leaders were subject to the same constraints facing any union leader. Further, their very differences from the "average guy" were penalized; they required more strength to act upon their convictions, yet they possessed less strength.

A change in the personnel of union leadership would, then, have very little effect upon policy. It would, paradoxically, have the most effect upon those unions which are autocratically controlled. Even in these, however, the leader acts within rigid limits. Important changes in policy will result only from changes in the role system of union leadership groups; roles, in turn, are based upon the necessary sources of power for the union, and these are not easily modified. It is unlikely that basic changes will result from educational programs for the members or the hiring of college graduates for the staff (not that these actions would not be desirable in themselves). Only if such moves have the final effect of changing the political structure will they be important. It is easy for any leader to behave in a democratic fashion, allowing power to the members and responding to their interests, in certain local unions: he must do so. On the other hand, it is doubtful if anyone could remain a leader in some locals if he insisted on democratic processes in the making of important decisions.

The same set of propositions applies to the commitment of leaders on the race issue. The attitudes of local union leaders is not the cause of ethnic inequality; it is the structure of action through which these attitudes must flow to be effective which perpetuates the *status quo.* Or, as one leader summed it up,

"Race is not usually an issue in the union movement."

APPENDICES

APPENDIX A

TABULAR MATERIALS

TABLE I

Proportions of Ethnic Minorities in the Memberships* of Twenty-Eight International Unions in Los Angeles County

LABOR UNION	Total Members	Total Ethnic	Mexi-can	Negro	Jewish	Other Ethnic
Service and Clerical						
Bartenders	6,000	.04	.01	---	.02	**
Waiters	4,000	.19	.02	.02	.15	---
Waitresses	8,100	.06	.01	.01	.03	.01[c]
Retail Clerks	15,000	.31	.07	.04	.13	.04[b]
Utility (Clerical)	250	.73	.01	---	.72	---.03[a]
Teamster #2 (Clerical)	650	.01	.01	---	---	---
Teamster #1	2,800	.14	.10	.02	.02	---
Communications Workers	6,500	.04	---	.04	---	**
Total	43,300					
Unweighted Average		.19	.03	.01	.13	**
Craftsman's Unions						
Painters	11,700	.43	.20	.03	.20	---
Cooks	5,850	.08	.03	.02	---	.03[d]
Plasterers	400	.43	.10	---	.07	.25[a]
Cement Finishers	1,000	.70	.50	.20	---	---
Total	18,950					
Unweighted Average		.41	.21	.06	.07	.07

* Data refer to entire membership in County with these exceptions: Teamsters, Lumber and Sawmill, north of Compton Boulevard only; Cement Finishers, Building Laborers, metropolitan center only.

** Less than .01.

[a] Italian

[b] Japanese

[c] Slav

[d] Filipino

TABLE I (continued)

LABOR UNION	Total Members	Total Ethnic	Mexi-can	Negro	Jewish	Other Ethnic
Industrial						
Auto Workers	50,000	.20	.10	.10	---	---
Steel Workers	16,000	.30	.20	.10	---	---
Utility Workers (Physical)	4,250	.13	.11	.02	---	---
Shipyard Workers	1,200	.24	.12	.12	---	---
Packinghouse (CIO) Workers	3,000	.66	.33	.33	---	---
Furniture Workers (CIO)	2,000	.70	.48	.20	.02	---
Rubber Workers	8,500	.20	.10	.10	---	---
Textile Workers	800	.50	.20	.20	.10	---
Oil Workers	5,500	.01	**	**	---	---
Mine, Mill, and Smelter	2,100	.41	.19	.22	---	---
Lumber and Saw-mill Workers	4,800	.42	.23	.09	---	.08[a]/ .02[c]
International Ladies Garment Work-ers Union	4,250	.93	.44	.27	.06	.11[b] .04[a]
United Brick and Clay Workers	3,200	.46	.25	.21	---	---
Packinghouse (AFL) Workers	1,800	.65	.41	.13	.01	.10[a]
Furniture Work-ers (AFL)	2,000	.60	.50	.10	---	---
Total	109,400					
Unweighted Average		.43	.25	.15	.01	.02
One-Job Unions						
Longshoremen	8,000	.43	.17	.16	---	.10[a]
Building Laborer	10,000	.76	.37	.39	---	---
Teamster #2 (Physical)	1,175	.27	.15	.12	---	---
Building Service Workers	7,000	.47	.07	.38	.01	.01[a]
Dishwashers	5,200	.39	.38	.01	---	---
Total	31,375					
Unweighted Average		.46	.23	.21	---	.02[a]

TABLE II

Proportion of the Membership Ethnic in Twenty-One Local Unions

LOCAL UNION	Total Members	Mexi-cans	Negroes	Other Ethnic	Non-Ethnic
Retail Clerks	15,100	.07	.04	.20	.69
Teamster #1 (Local Freight)	2,830	.10	.02	.02	.86
Teamster #2 Ware-housemen(Clerks)	1,825	.10	.07	---	.83
Cement Finishers	1,000	.50	.20	---	.30
Plasterers	400	.10	---	.25	.65
Mine, Mill and Smelter Workers	2,050	.17	.22	---	.61
Furniture Workers, Independent	2,055	.48	.20	.02	.30
Utility Workers	1,500	.33	.06	.10	.50
Steel Workers	800	.41	.04	---	.55
Packinghouse Work-ers (CIO)	260	.19	.38	---	.43
Furniture Workers (CIO)	1,738	.49	.04	.03	.44
Textile Workers	800	.20	.20	.10	.50
Shipyard Workers	1,200	.12	.12	---	.76
Lumber and Saw-mill Workers	4,675	.23	.09	.08	.60
International Ladies Garment Workers Union	4,220	.44	.27	.21	.08

TABLE II (continued)

Local Union	Total Members	Mexi-cans	Negroes	Other Ethnic	Non-Ethnic
Packinghouse Workers (AFL)	1,800	.41	.13	.10	.36
Furniture Workers (AFL)	2,000	.50	.10	---	.40
United Brick and Clay Workers	180	.60	.28	---	.12
Building Laborers	10,000	.37	.39	---	.34
Building Service Workers #1 (Downtown)	5,450	.09	.50	.15	.26
Building Service Workers #2 (Hollywood)	410	.02	.48	.10	.40

TABLE III

Proportion of Members Attending General Membership* Meetings, with Indexes of Attendance for Three Populations

Local Union	Prop'n. of Total Members	Index of Attendance Mexican	Negroes	Other
Customer Service and Craft				
Teamster #1	.12	83	42	108
Teamster #2 Warehousemen and Clerks	.05	80	100	100
Cement Finishers	.06	00	350	133
Plasterers	.12	42	---	108
Industrial				
steel Workers	.11	109	27	100
Utility Workers	.06	16	80	133
Furniture Workers (CIO)	.16	106	94	81
Packinghouse Workers	.16	26	200	50
Mine, Mill, and Smelter Workers (Independent)	.05	140	100	100
Furniture Workers (Independent)	.10	40	250	100
Industrial				
Lumber and Sawmill Workers	.09	110	100	100
United Brick and Clay Workers	.44	70	57	113
International Ladies Garment Workers Union	.20	60	100	---
Furniture Workers (AFL)	.04	100	100	100

* Retail Clerks and Packinghouse Workers AFL omitted (fined meetings only); Textile Workers and Shipyard Workers omitted, data inadequate.

TABLE III (continued)

Local Union	Prop'n of Total Members	Index of Attendance Mexican	Negroes	Other
One-job				
Building Laborers	.02	125	125	50
Building Service Workers #1 (Downtown)	.02	50	100	200
Building Service Workers #2 (Hollywood)	.15	000	120	33
Unweighted Average, All Locals	.11	67	124	99
Customer Service and Craft plus One-job locals	.08	54	139	105
Industrial locals	.14	77	114	95

TABLE IV

The Leadership Population of Twenty-one Local Unions with the Proportions of Ethnic Officers

Type of Local	Total Members	Chief Stewards	Ex. Bd. Members	Staff Officers
Craft and Customer Service				
Mexican	.10	.46	.02	.08
Negro	.04	.07	.02	.04
Other	.86	.47	.96	.88
	1.00	1.00	1.00	1.00
Number	21,000	115	51	25
Industrial (CIO)				
Mexican	.32	.30	.19	.25
Negro	.14	.14	.14	.12
Other	.54	.56	.67	.63
	1.00	1.00	1.00	1.00
Number	10,350	211	197	16
Industrial (AFL)				
Mexican	.40	.22	.17	.11
Negro	.19	.24	.10	.00
Other	.41	.54	.63	.89
	1.00	1.00	1.00	1.00
Number	12,400	189	113	17
One-job Laborer				
Mexicans	.22	.25	.28	.33
Negroes	.35	.47	.31	.19
Others	.43	.28	.41	.48
	1.00	1.00	1.00	1.00
Number	19,350	330	36	21

TABLE IV (continued)

Type of Local	Total Members	Chief Stewards	Ex. Bd. Members	Staff Officers
Total: All Locals				
Mexicans	.23	.28	.18	.19
Negroes	.17	.28	.13	.09
Others	.60	.44	.69	.72
	1.00	1.00	1.00	1.00
Number	63,000	845	397	79

TABLE V

Representation Index for Ethnic Minorities at Three Levels in the Formal Structure of the Locals*

Local Union	MEXICANS Stew.	Ex. Bd.	Staff	NEGROES Stew.	Ex. Bd.	Staff
Customer Service and Craft Workers						
Retail Clerks	---	-.07[a]	-.07	---	1.00	1.50
Teamster #1	2.00	-.10	-.10	6.00[b]	-.02	-.02
Plasterers	---	.70	10.00[b]	---	---	---
Cement Finishers	1.00	.40	.50	.30	-.20	-.20
Industrial						
Utility Workers	.75	-.33	-.33	4.28[b]	-.07	-.07
Steel Workers	.61	.73	2.45[b]	-.04	-.04	-.04
Furniture Workers (CIO)	.51	.51	1.34	1.00	3.00[b]	-.04
Packinghouse Workers (CIO)	.42	.47	-.33[c]	1.65	.94	1.51[c]
Shipyard Workers	1.33	2.08	-.12	1.33	1.83	-.12
Textile Workers	1.80	1.10	-.20	.45	1.10	-.20

* Index = proportion ethnic officers as a fraction of proportion of ethnic members in the local.

[a] The proportion of members who are ethnic and have no representation in an office is given a negative sign and included; it is not an index.

[b] Extreme figures indicate small number of ethnic members in local.

[c] No local staff; computed on a regional basis as an approximation.

TABLE V (continued)

Local Union	MEXICANS			NEGROES		
	Stew.	Ex. Bd.	Staff	Stew.	Ex. Bd.	Staff
Furniture Workers (Independent)	1.29	.30	.33	.10	.40	.80
Mine, Mill and Smelter Workers (Independent)	.94	1.00	-.17	.72	.77	1.13
Packinghouse Workers(AFL)	1.00	.26	-.41	.61	-.13	-.13
Lumber and Sawmill Workers	.52	-.23	-.23	-.10	-.10	-.10
Furniture Workers (AFL)	.92	.72	.66	.60	-.10	-.10
International Ladies Garment Workers Union	.22	.44	.28	1.48	.74	-.27
United Brick and Clay Workers	.54	1.23	1.00[c]	1.22	.45	-.21[c]
One-job Laborer						
Building Laborers	.94	1.21	1.14	1.02	.92	.92
Building Service Workers #1 (Downtown)	1.00	3.33[b]	3.50[b]	1.00	.12	.20
Building Service Workers #2	-.02	-.02	-.02	1.04	1.04	-.48

TABLE VI

Ethnic Proportions of the Membership and Officers in Thirteen Industrial Locals

Local Union	Members	Stewards	Ex. Bd.	Staff
A. Plant Oriented				
Steelworkers				
Number	(800)	(35)	(60)	(1)
Mexicans	.41	.27	.30	1.00
Negroes	.03	---	---	---
Furniture Workers (CIO)				
Number	(1738)	(23)	(33)	(3)
Mexicans	.49	.25	.25	.67
Negroes	.04	.04	.12	---
Textile Workers				
Number	(800)	(11)	(22)	(3)
Mexicans	.20	.36	.22	---
Negroes	.20	.09	.22	---
Mine, Mill and Smelter Workers				
Number	(2100)	(30)	(40)	(4)
Mexicans	.17	.16	.17	---
Negroes	.22	.16	.17	.25
Packinghouse Workers (CIO)				
Number	(260)	(13)	(11)	(2)*
Mexicans	.19	.08	.09	---
Negroes	.38	.63	.36	.50
Shipyard Workers				
Number	(1200)	(50)	(28)	(1)
Mexicans	.12	.16	.25	---
Negroes	.12	.16	.22	---
United Brick and Clay Workers				
Number	(180)	(3)	(8)	(4)*
Mexicans	.60	.33	.75	.25
Negroes	.28	.33	.12	---

* No local staff: computed on regional basis.

TABLE VI (continued)

Local Union	Members	Stewards	Ex. Bd.	Staff
B. Hall-Oriented				
Utility Workers				
Number	(1500)	(19)	(15)	(1)
Mexicans	.33	.25	---	---
Negroes	.06	.30	---	---
Furniture Workers (AFL)				
Number	(2000)	(36)	(11)	(3)
Mexicans	.50	.46	.36	.33
Negroes	.10	.06	---	---
Lumber and Sawmill Workers				
Number	(4637)	(25)	(15)	(5)
Mexicans	.23	.12	---	---
Negroes	.10	---	---	---
Packinghouse Workers (AFL)				
Number	(1700)	(25)	(9)	(2)
Mexicans	.41	.40	.11	---
Negroes	.13	.08	---	---
Furniture Workers (Ind.)				
Number	(1950)	(48)	(13)	(5)
Mexicans	.48	.62	.15	.16
Negroes	.20	.02	.08	.16
ILGWU				
Number	(4500)	(100)	(25)	(8)
Mexicans	.44	.10	.20	.12
Negroes	.27	.40	.20	---

APPENDIX B

BIBLIOGRAPHY

BIBLIOGRAPHY

1. American Civil Liberties Union, Democracy in Trade Unions: A Survey with a Program of Action. New York: American Civil Liberties Union, 1943.

2. Bailer, Loyd H., "Organized Labor and Racial Minorities," Annals of the American Academy of Political and Social Science, Vol. 274, March, 1951, pp. 101-107.

3. Bloom, Leonard and Riemer, Ruth, Removal and Return, The Socio-Economic Effects of the War on Japanese Americans, Berkeley and Los Angeles: University of California Press, 1949.

4. Blumer, Herbert, "Public Opinion and the Public Opinion Polls," American Sociological Review, Vol. XIII, No. 5, October, 1948, pp. 542-549.

5. Committee on Mexican Labor in California, Report (The Governor Young Report), Sacramento: 1930.

6. Cayton , Horace R., Black Workers and the New Unions, Chapel Hill: University of North Carolina Press, 1939.

7. Cottrell, Edwin A. and Jones, Helen L., Metropolitan Los Angeles, A Study in Integration: Vol. I, Characteristics of the Metropolis, Los Angeles: The Haynes Foundation, 1952.

8. Dalton, Melville, "Unofficial Union-Management Relations," American Sociological Review, Vol. XV, No. 5, October, 1950, pp. 611-619.

9. Dotson, Floyd, "Voluntary Associations in Mexico City," American Sociological Review, Vol. XVIII, No. 4, August, 1953, pp. 380-386.

10. Drucker, Peter, The New Society: The Anatomy of Industrial Order, New York: Harper and Brothers, 1950.

11. Edwards, Alba M., A Socio-Economic Grouping of the Gainful Workers of the United States, Washington, D. C.: U. S. Government Printing Office, 1938.

12. Frazier, E. Franklin, "Race Contacts and the Social Structure," _American Sociological Review_, Vol. XIV, No. 1, February, 1949, pp. 1-11.

13. Gordon, Margaret S., _Employment Expansion and Population Growth, The California Experience: 1900-1950_, Berkeley and Los Angeles: University of California Press, 1954.

14. Greer, Scott, _Social Organization_, New York: Doubleday and Company, 1955.

15. ________________, "Situational Pressures and Functional Role of the Ethnic Labor Leader," _Social Forces_, Vol. XXXII, No. 1, October, 1953, pp. 41-45.

16. ________________, "The Participation of Ethnic Minorities in the Labor Unions of Los Angeles County," unpublished Ph. D. dissertation, University of California, Los Angeles, 1952.

17. ________________, and Baggish, Henry, "Chavez Ravine: Urbanization and Occupational Mobility in a Mexican-American Enclave," unpublished research report, Department of Anthropology, University of California, Los Angeles, 1949.

18. Herberg, Will, "Bureaucracy and Democracy in Trade Unions," _Antioch Review_, Vol. III, September, 1943, pp. 405-417.

19. Howe, Irving and Widick, B. J., _The U.A.W. and Walter Reuther_, New York: Random House, 1949.

20. Johnson, Malcolm Malone, _Crime on the Labor Front_, New York: McGraw-Hill, 1950.

21. Kidner, Frank L. and Neff, Philip, _An Economic Survey of the Los Angeles Area_, Los Angeles: The Haynes Foundation, 1945.

22. Lindblom, Charles Edward, _Unions and Captalism_, New Haven: Yale University Press, 1949.

23. Lipset, Seymour M., Martin Trow and James Coleman _Union Democracy: The Internal Politics of the International Typographical Union_, Glencoe, Illinois: The Free Press, 1956.

24. Los Angeles County Conference on Employment, Proceedings, Los Angeles, 1950.

25. Mannheim, Karl, Ideology and Utopia, New York: Harcourt, Brace, and Company, 1936.

26. Mills, C. Wright, (with the assistance of Helen Schneider), The New Men of Power, America's Labor Leaders, New York: Harcourt-Brace, 1948.

27. Myrdal, Gunnar, An American Dilemma, New York: Harper and Brothers, 1944,

28. North, Cecil, and Hatt, Paul K., "Jobs and Occupations, a Popular Evaluation," Opinion News, September 1, 1947, pp. 3-13.

29. Northrup, Herbert R., Organized Labor and the Negro, New York and London: Harper and Brothers, 1944.

30. Roeshlisberger, F.J. and Dickson, William J., Management and the Worker, Cambridge: Harvard University Press, 1939. .

31. Rose, Caroline, "Morale in a Trade Union," American Journal of Sociology, Vol. LVI, No. 2, September, 1950, pp. 167-174.

32. Ross, Arthur, Trade Union Determinants of Industrial Wage Policy, Berkeley and Los Angeles: University of California Press, 1949.

33. Sayles, Leonard R. and Strauss, George, The Local Union: Its Place in the Industrial Plant, New York: Harper and Brothers, 1953.

34. Seidman, Joel, London, Jack and Karsh, Bernard, "Why Workers Join Unions," Annals of the American Academy of Political and Social Science, Vol. 274, March, 1951, pp. 75-85.

35. Selznick, Philip, "Foundations of the Theory of Organization," American Sociological Review, Vol. XIII, No. 1, February, 1948, pp. 25-35.

36. Slichter, Sumner H., The Challenge of Industrial Relations, Ithaca, New York: Cornell University Press, 1947.

37. Shevky, Eshref and Williams, Marilyn, The Social Areas of Los Angeles, Berkeley and Los Angeles: University of California Press, 1949.

38. Thompson, Warren S., The Population of California, 1850-1950, Los Angeles: The Haynes Foundation, 1955.

39. Tannenbaum, Frank, A Philosophy of Labor, New York: Alfred A. Knopf, 1951.

40. Wilensky, Harold, Intellectuals in the Labor Unions, Glencoe, Illinois: The Free Press, 1956.